Floral Craft for Weddings

Floral Craft for Weddings

Margo-Ann Daly

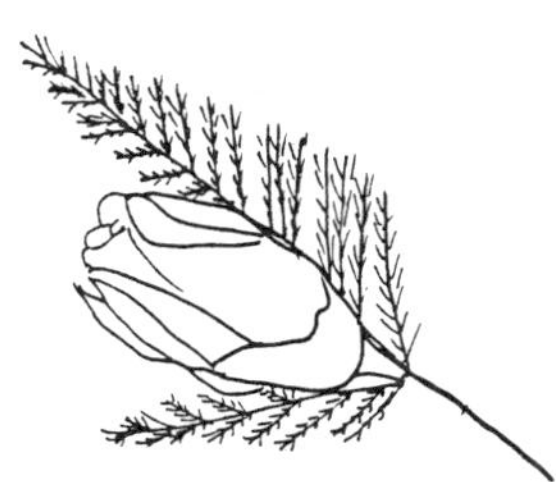

Kangaroo Press

Acknowledgments

Many thanks to those who helped in the creation of this book, with special thanks to Vicky, Jasmine and Tarynne.

Floral and headwear arrangements by Margo-Ann Daly.
Drawings by Philip Daly.
Photography by Steve Norris from Souvenir Studio, Katoomba.
Wedding hire accessories from Park Hire, South Nowra.

First published in 1995 by Kangaroo Press Pty Ltd
3 Whitehall Road Kenthurst NSW 2156 Australia
PO Box 6125 Dural Delivery Centre NSW 2158
Typeset in Australia by Lynwood Press, Kulnura
Printed in Hong Kong through Colorcraft Ltd

ISBN 0 86417 683 X

Contents

Introduction

Floral work for special occasions is very satisfying. This book is designed to give you some of the basic techniques of floral work to enable you to create your own bouquets and headwear for weddings. I have tried not to go into too many technical details but rather to keep things fairly simple.

Most of the bridal accessories I have chosen are fairly inexpensive to make, as cost becomes a major concern when arranging a wedding. Both fresh and artificial flowers can be used.

The book covers all floral aspects of a wedding, from the bridal bouquets to the flowergirls' baskets, headwear for the bride and bridesmaids, corsages and other trimmings and flowers for the reception.

Margo-Ann

Bouquets and baskets

Equipment

Florist's wire: 22, 24 and 26 gauge
Millinery wire
Wire cutters
Scissors
Florist's tape (green and white)
Pearl-headed pins (optional)
Clear craft glue
Oasis ball or block
Various bowls
Lace posy frill (optional)
Florist's ribbon or satin ribbon
Plastic hair bands and combs
Flowergirls' baskets

Wiring and taping techniques

The two main styles of wiring used in this book are *single leg wiring* for bouquets and headpieces, and *double leg wiring* for baskets and table arrangements. With artificial flowers it is not crucial to wire them exactly whereas fresh flowers are delicate and need special wiring techniques.

Taping Acquiring the knack of taping using Parafilm (florist's tape) is just a matter of practice, of stretching the tape and twisting the wire at the same time. If you find this a little difficult at first, stretch 5 cm (2'') of tape out to about 10 cm (4'') first, then twist it around the wire. You must stretch the tape as otherwise it becomes too thick and bulky. Practice the technique with a few pieces of plain wire before starting on flowers and leaves.

Single leg wiring for bouquets and headpieces
Use 22 gauge wire for bouquets; 24 and 26 gauge wire for headpieces.

Individual leaves (e.g. gum and ivy)
With the back of the leaf facing you, thread a 22 gauge wire through the leaf, around the spine and back out again, twisting the longer wire around the stem and shorter wire, and bind together with florist's tape. See diagrams 1 and 2.

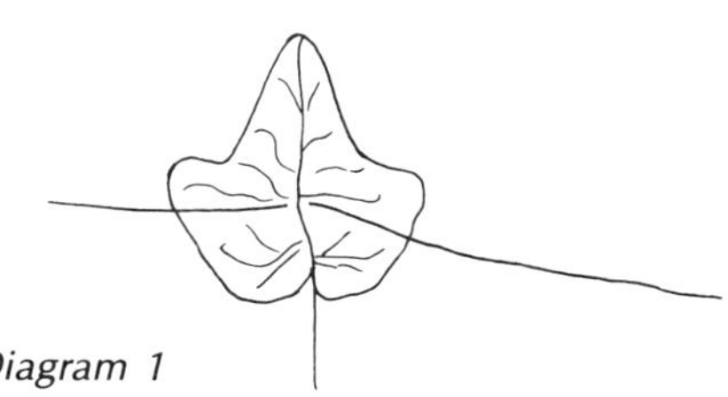

Diagram 1

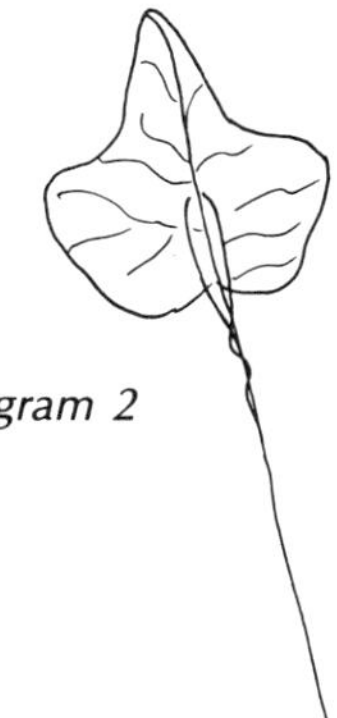

Diagram 2

Dried gum stem Using a 22 gauge wire, hook it around the first set of leaves on the stem, then bring it down, twist it around the shorter wire and the stem and bind with florist's tape. See diagram 3.

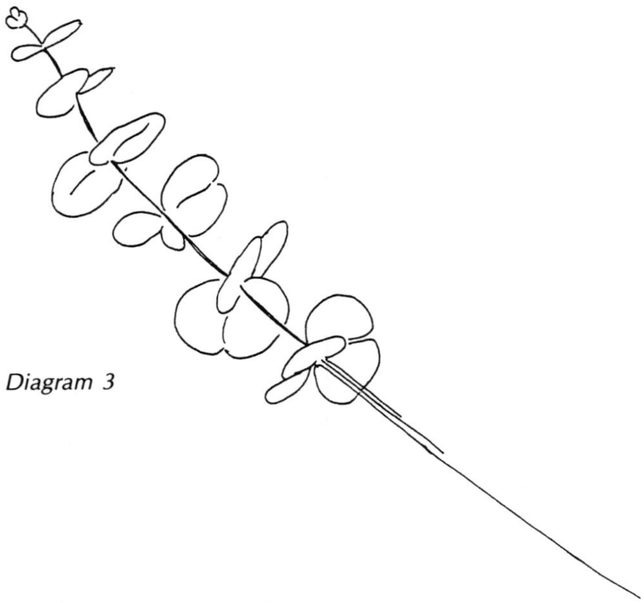

Diagram 3

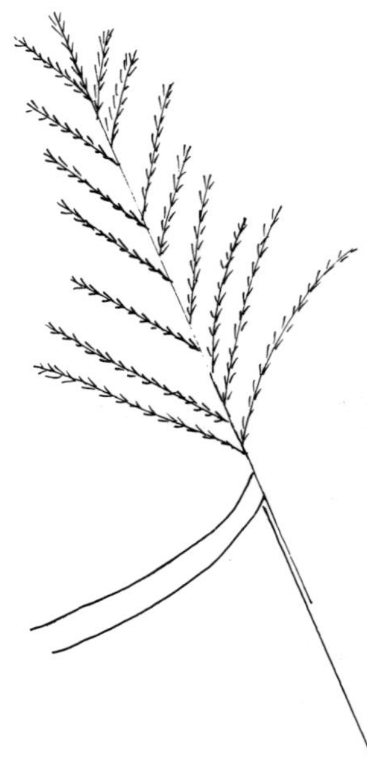

Diagram 5

Artificial foliage (e.g. fern, ivy)
As the stems of artificial foliage are usually plastic and fairly strong, lay a 22 gauge wire parallel to the stem and bind together with florist's tape. See diagrams 4 and 5.

Diagram 4

Dried baby's breath Lay a 24 gauge wire with a long hook at one end against the bunch of baby's breath and twist the longer part of the wire around the baby's breath and the shorter wire. See diagrams 6 and 7.

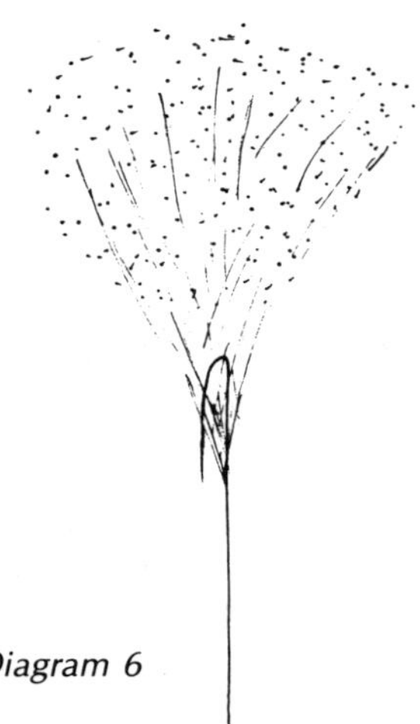

Diagram 6

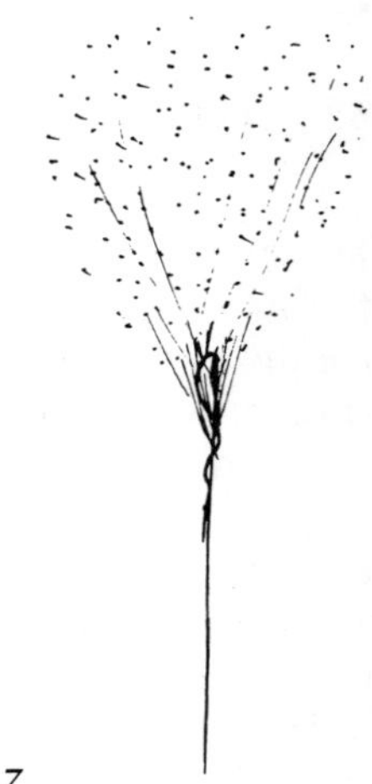

Diagram 7

A traditional posy of cream and apricot roses and dried baby's breath finished off with dried gum and apricot bows (page 14)

Rose and ivy corsage (page 37), rose and fern corsage (page 38) and rose and carnation buttonholes (page 39)

Equipment for floral work includes florist's wire, millinery wire, wire cutters, scissors, florist's tape, pearl-headed pins, glue, Oasis balls, fine paper-covered wire, various bowls, lace posy frill, satin ribbon, plastic hair band, flowergirls' baskets, cardboard cylinder and wooden dowel

Equipment for headwear includes millinery wire, scissors, glue, wire cutters, tailor's chalk, 32 gauge brass wire, white florist's tape, a thin metal band, 26 gauge florist's wire, needle and cotton

Flowers used in bouquets and floral head-pieces include medium roses, mini roses, moth orchids, bell flowers, gladiolus, stock and chrysanthemums

Below left:
Foliages used in the pieces in this book include artificial fern, dried gum, ivy and dried baby's breath

Below:
Flowers used in the sheaf bouquet *(see page 17)*

An informal bouquet of moth orchids, medium roses, ivy and fern (page 15)

Artificial flowers (e.g. roses, carnations) Remove the artificial stem and insert a 22 gauge wire stem with a hook at one end, first adding a liberal amount of glue, and reattach the flower. Bind the wire stem and plastic casing with florist's tape. See diagrams 8 and 9.

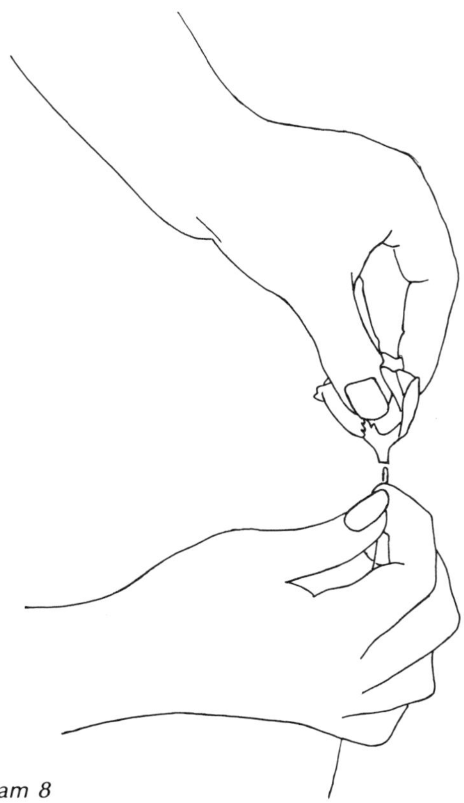

Diagram 8

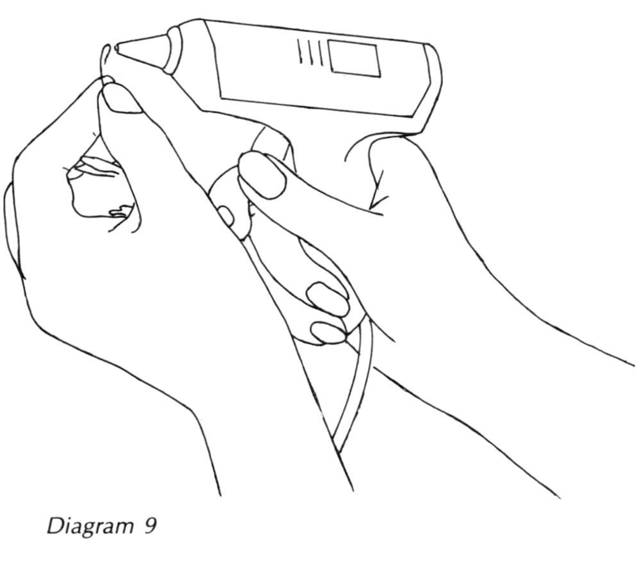

Diagram 9

Double leg wiring for baskets and table arrangements

Most artificial flowers and some foliage have very strong stems which don't need to be replaced. To stop the flower coming off just apply glue to the stem and insert it back into the flower head.

If you need to add a new wire stem follow the same general instructions for single leg wiring. The only difference is that the wire ends are the same length, which gives added strength for baskets and arrangements. See diagrams 10 and 11.

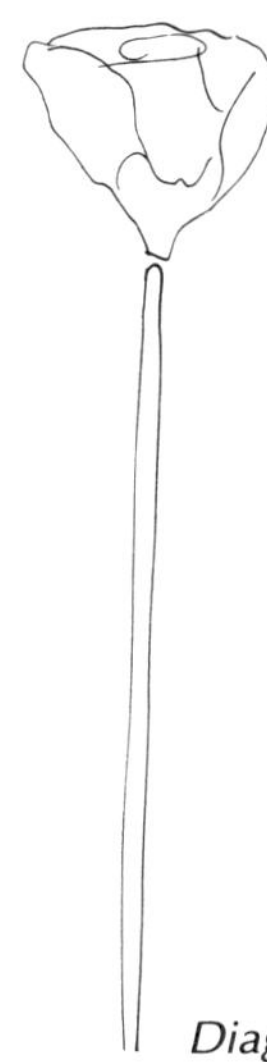

Diagram 10

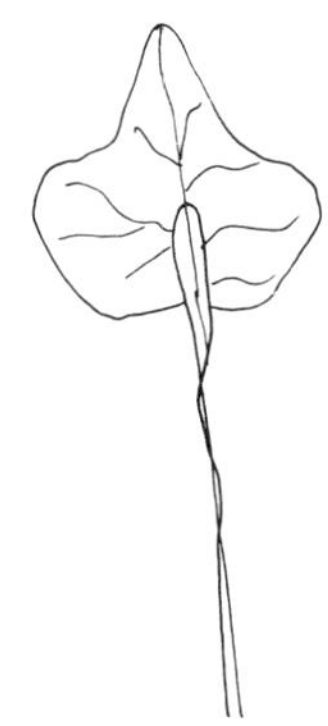

Diagram 11

Bridal flowers (with fine wire stems) Use the same method as for artificial foliage, laying a 24 gauge wire against the fine wire stem and binding with florist's tape. See diagram 12.

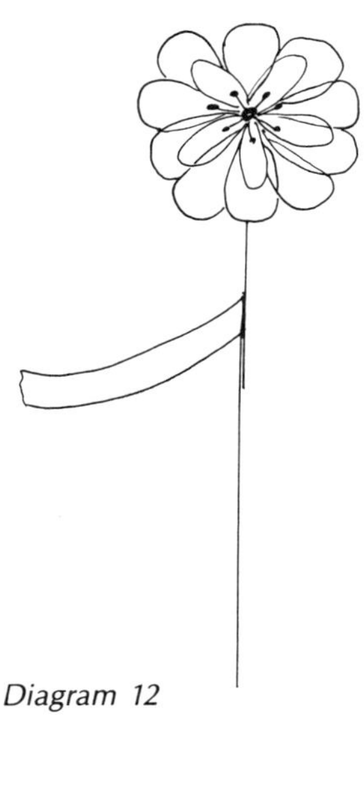

Diagram 12

Traditional posy

Materials
25 medium to large cream roses
11 small to medium apricot roses
2 stems of bell flowers (makes 20 small bunches)
16 dried gum stems
dried baby's breath (instead of bell flowers)
florist's tape
22 gauge wire
2 m (2½ yds) cream ribbon

Diagram 2

Method

1. Wire all flowers and foliage following the guidelines on pages 7–13, cutting gum stems to about 10 cm (4").
2. Take one cream rose as the centre flower, add three bunches bell flowers, three gum stems and three apricot roses. Tape them together about 10 cm (4") down from the base of the centre flower, cutting off excess wire as you go. See diagram 1.

Diagram 3

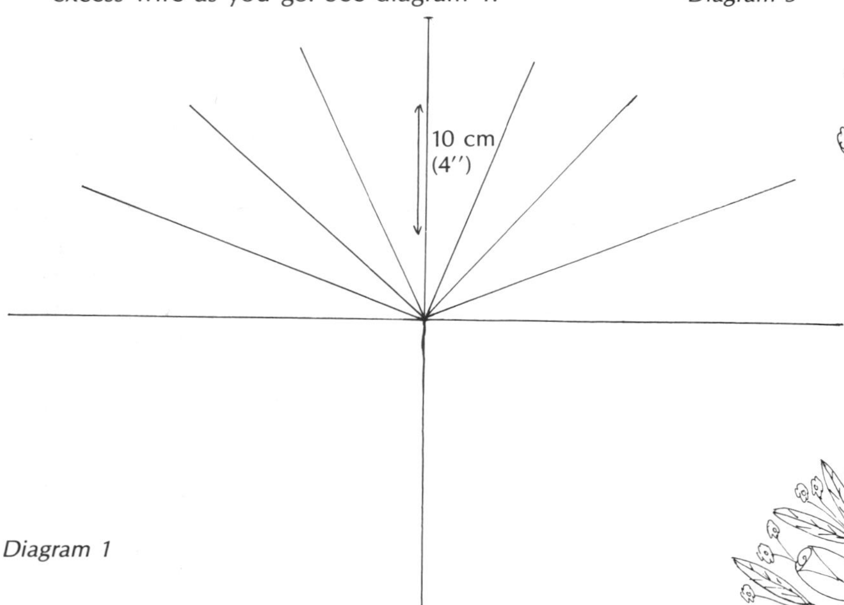

Diagram 1

3. For the second row place eight cream roses evenly around the central roses. See diagram 2.
4. In the third row place eight apricot roses evenly around the posy with bell flowers and gum stems taped together. See diagram 3.
5. Make the final row with the sixteen remaining cream roses, bell flowers and gum stems, extending the flowers and foliage stems out to accommodate the width of the posy. Tape together. See diagram 4.
6. To tidy up the posy handle, cut off any excess wire 10 cm (4") below the base of the flowers and re-tape. Add ribbon streamer to handle if desired.

Diagram 4

Informal bouquet

Materials
9 pink roses
7 orchids
6 sprigs of ivy
2 bunches of fern (makes 20 sprigs)
13 stephanotis
florist's tape
22 gauge wire
2 m (2½ yds) ribbon

Method
1. Wire all flowers and foliage following the guidelines on pages 7–13.
2. Group orchids in a random pattern as in diagram 1.
3. Place roses and stephanotis in and around the orchids as in diagram 2.
4. Add sprigs of fern in between the orchids and roses; this helps hide the wire stems and gives it a fuller, more natural look.
5. To tidy the back of the posy, position about ten sprigs of fern and six sprigs of ivy evenly around the posy, taping in place; this hides the wire stems from the back and looks more professional.
6. Finish off by taping ribbon streamer to posy handle if desired.

Diagram 1

Diagram 2

Back view of the informal bouquet, showing how it is finished off with artificial fern for a more professional touch

Traditional trail bouquet

Materials
24 medium to large cream roses
15 small to medium apricot roses
5 small to medium cream roses
3 stems bell flowers
25 dried gum stems
5 dried gum leaves with stem
green florist's tape
22 gauge florist's wire
2 m (2½ yds) cream ribbon

Method
1. Wire and tape all flowers and foliage following the guidelines on pages 7–13.
2. Construct a traditional posy following the instructions on page 14.
3. To make the trail, take an individual wired leaf, place a bunch of bell flowers against it and tape them together. Place two leaves and a cream rose above the first leaf, and tape in place. See diagram 1.
4. Place the next four roses plus bell flowers and two leaves and tape together. See diagram 2.
5. Continue to the end of the trail with the next eight roses, leaves and bell flowers, extending the length of each wire stem before taping. See diagram 3.
6. To tape the trail to the posy, cut excess wire off the trail to about 15 cm (6″) and bend the trail slightly. Place the trail against the posy stem and tape together. See diagram 4.
7. To finish off, tape ribbon streamers to stem.

Diagram 3

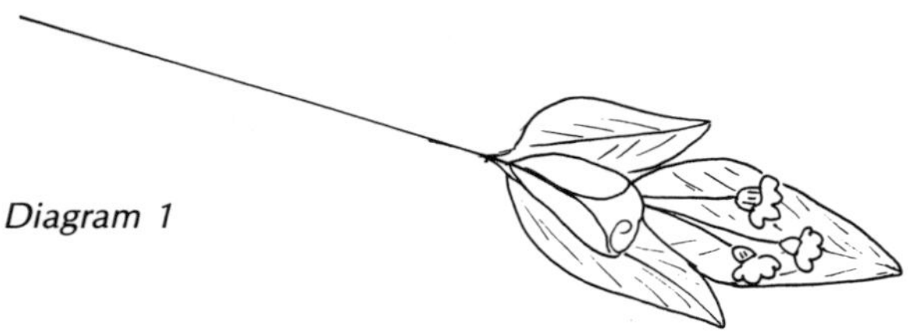

Diagram 1

Diagram 2

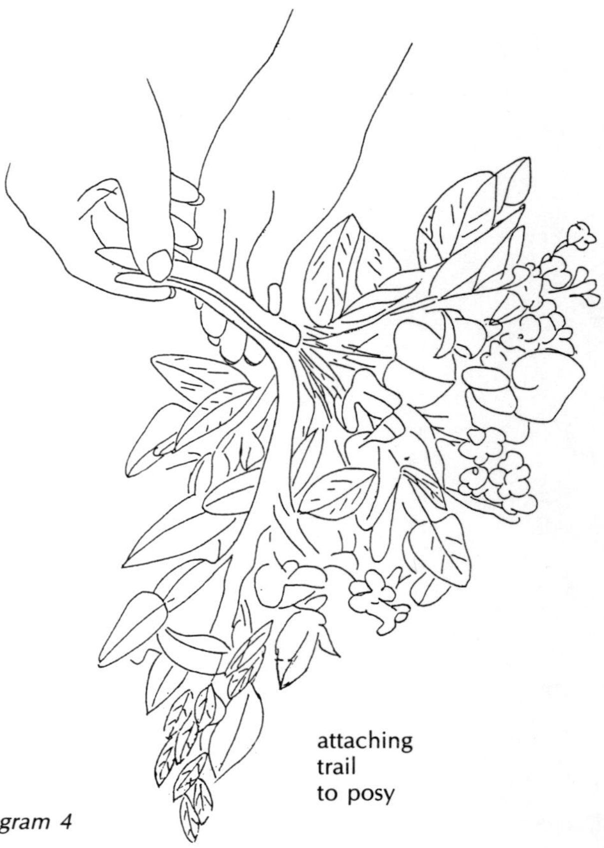

Diagram 4

Sheaf bouquet

Materials

5 sprigs of gum with long stems
5 gladioli stems
3 stocks (or similar flowers)
9 chrysanthemums
5 roses
fine tie wire
1 m x 2.5 cm (39'' x 1'') cream satin ribbon
sticky tape
1 pearl-headed pin
wire cutters
1 cream satin bow

Method

1. If you are using artificial flowers there is no need to re-wire the stems as they are excellent for this bouquet.
2. Lay the five sprigs of gum evenly on a flat surface, and lay the five gladioli and three stocks in between the gum.
3. Place six chrysanthemums about 30 cm (12'') down from the top of the bouquet, spacing them evenly.
4. Place five roses evenly just under the chrysanthemum flowers, then finish off with three chrysanthemums. See diagram 1.
5. Now bunch the flowers together and secure with wire, twisting around the base of the sheaf just below the last three flowers. See diagram 2.
6. At this point the flowers could well have moved from their original positions. Don't worry, just organise the flowers the best way you can as this bouquet doesn't need to be perfect.
7. To tidy up the stems, measure down 25 cm (10'') from the bases of the last three flowers and cut away excess wire stems evenly.

Diagram 1

Diagram 2

8. To apply the satin ribbon, start at the bottom of the stems, securing the end of the ribbon to the stems with sticky tape so it won't move. Wrap the ribbon around the stem two or three times to hide the sticky tape. Wind the ribbon spirally up the stem until you reach the base of the flowers, cut off excess and secure with a pearl-headed pin. See diagram 3.
9. Make a satin bow following the guidelines on pages 57–58.
10. Place the satin bow just below the three last flowers, loop the ribbon ties around the gum stems at the back of the bouquet and tie in a knot, then a bow. See diagram 4.

Diagram 3

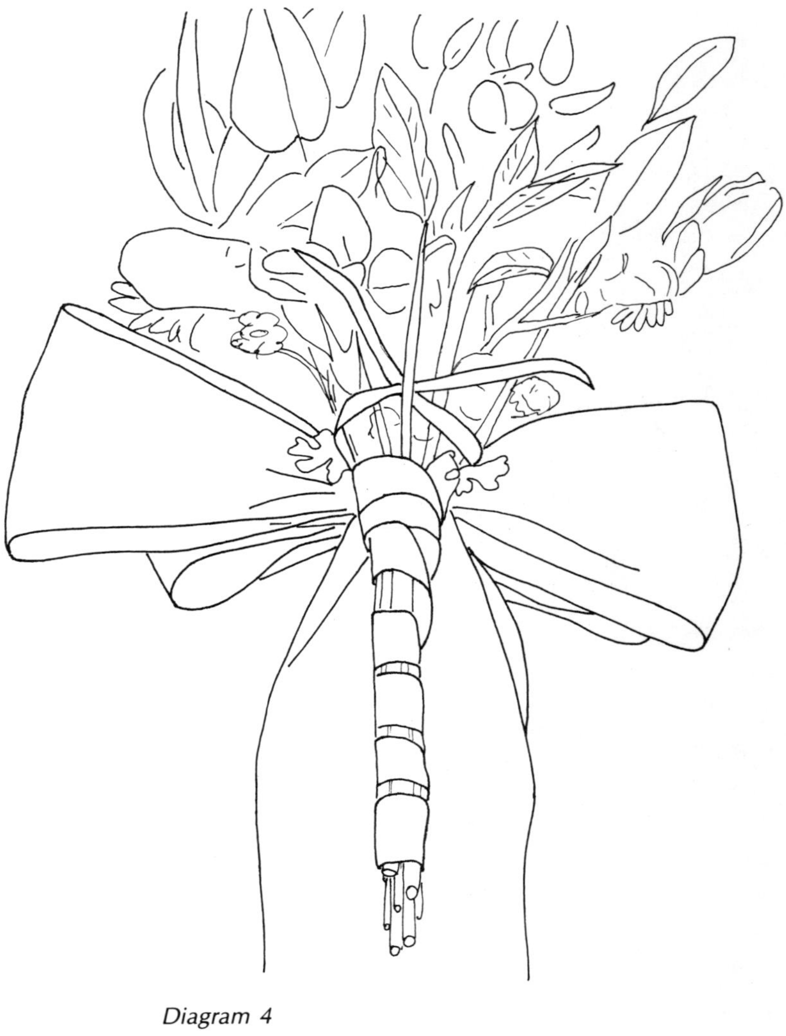

Diagram 4

Traditional flowergirl's basket

Materials

1 small flowergirl's basket
8 medium cream rosebuds
9 medium apricot rosebuds
12 individual gum leaves
10 ribbon bows
small block of Oasis
15 sprigs of dried baby's breath
3 m x 5 mm (3½ yds x ¼″) apricot ribbon
22 gauge wire
glue

Method

1. Wire all gum leaves and baby's breath. You can keep the original stems of the roses for this basket if you prefer.
2. Glue Oasis to the bottom of the basket and allow it to dry. Position the apricot roses in the Oasis following diagram 1.
3. Fill in the gaps with the cream roses. See diagram 2.
4. Place the gum leaves and ribbon bows in and around the roses. See diagram 3.
5. Now place the baby's breath in between the roses, leaves and bows to hide the Oasis.
6. Twist ribbon around the handle, gluing the ribbon at both sides of the handle to secure. Make one ribbon streamer and a six-loop ribbon bow, tape them together, twist around the side of the handle, and cut off excess wire. See diagram 4.

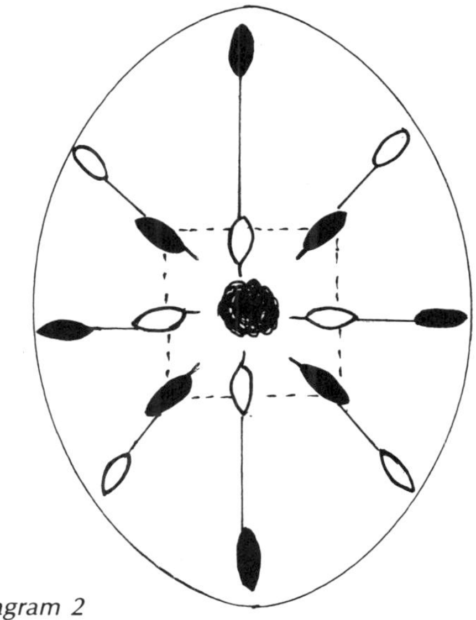

Diagram 2

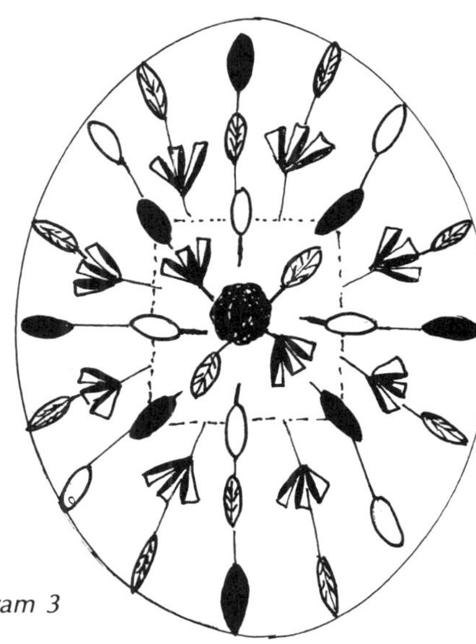

Diagram 3

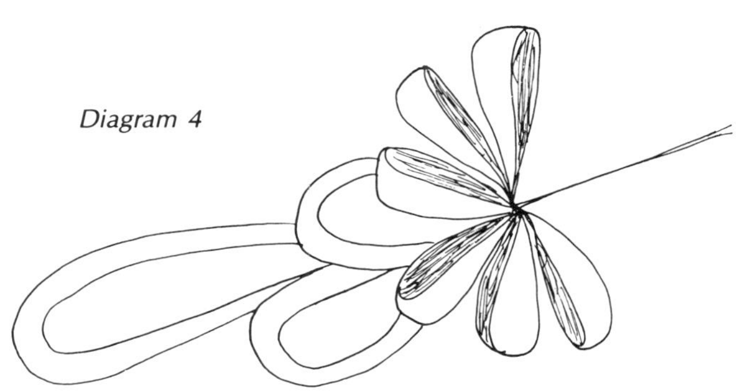

Diagram 4

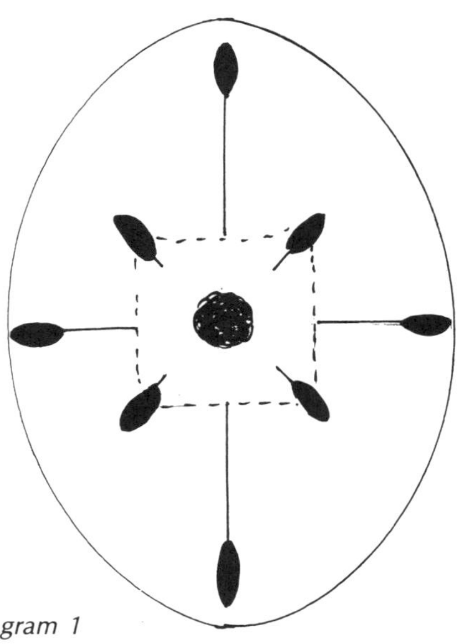

Diagram 1

Tulle flowergirl's basket

Materials
small flowergirl's basket
50 cm (20″) bridal tulle
one bunch forget-me-not
pearls (optional)
3 m x 5 mm (3½ yds x ¼″) narrow ribbon
needle and cotton

Method

1. Make a paper pattern the size of the basket.
2. Now fold the tulle in six to eight layers, pin the pattern to the tulle and cut around the pattern. See diagram 1.
3. With needle and cotton sew a running stitch through the centre of the layers of tulle, gather up the running stitch very tightly then sew to secure. See diagram 2.
4. The layers now have to be separated. Take the first two layers on one side and pull the tulle in the opposite direction. See diagram 3.
5. Apply glue to the base of the basket and glue the tulle ruffle in place.
6. Now glue forget-me-nots, pearls or other small flowers all over the tulle. See diagram 4.
7. To finish, bind the handle with ribbon and add a bow and streamers to one side of the basket.

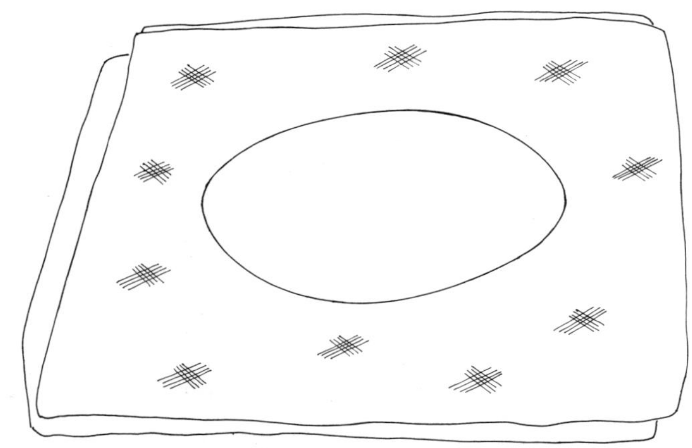

Diagram 1

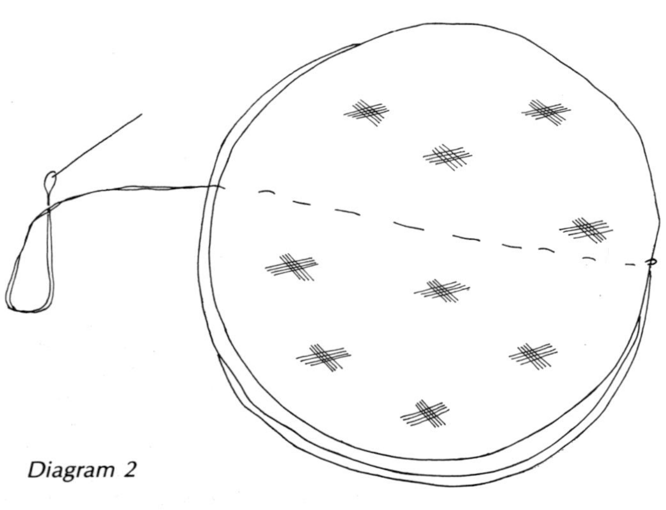

Diagram 2

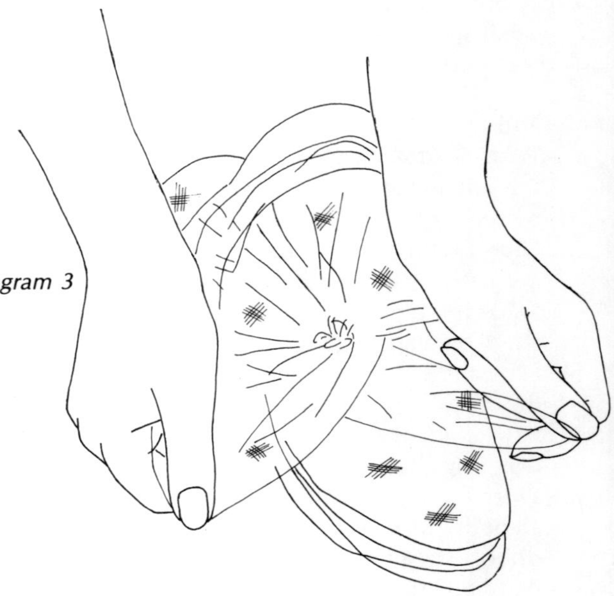

Diagram 3

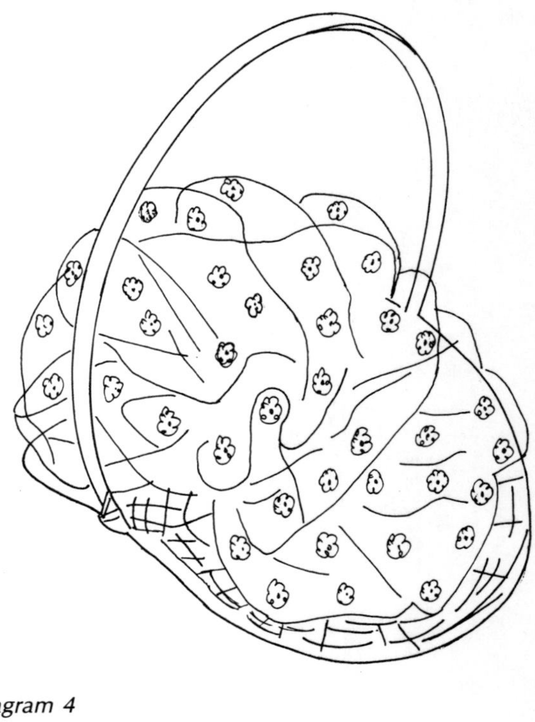

Diagram 4

A traditional trail bouquet of cream and apricot roses, bell flowers and dried gum (page 16)

A sheaf bouquet of gladiolus, stock, chrysanthemums, roses and dried gum, finished off with a large satin bow (page 17)

Traditional flowergirl's basket of small cream and apricot roses and dried baby's breath, finished off with apricot bows (page 19)

Rose petal basket edged with ribbon roses (page 25) and tulle flowergirl's basket filled with white tulle and spotted with pink forget-me-nots (page 20)

This delicate pearl loop tiara will complement any gown (page 26)

An exquisite plaited pearl tiara can be worn with or without a veil (page 28)

Rose petal basket

Materials

one medium dolly basket
one packet dried rose petals
25 cm x 25 cm (10'' x 10'') fine fabric
60 cm x 1 cm (24'' x ½'') lace
15 medium pink roses
15 medium white ribbon roses
2 bunches forget-me-nots (pink or white)
two bunches small leaves (optional)
1 m (39'') millinery wire
white or green florist's tape
1 roll 32 gauge brass wire

Method

1. Measure the circumference of the inner edge of the basket and cut the fabric slightly larger.
2. Apply glue to the inner edge of the basket, and glue fabric in place. To cover the raw edge, apply a line of glue along the edge and cover with lace. See diagram 1.
3. To make the ring of flowers to go around the basket, measure the circumference of the outer edge and add an extra 5 cm (2''); cut millinery wire to suit.
4. Now start with one bunch of forget-me-nots, then one white ribbon rose, one leaf, one bunch of forget-me-nots, one pink rose, one leaf, one bunch of forget-me-nots. Continue this pattern until you come to the end of the wire, leaving 5 cm (2'') of wire for joining. See diagram 2.
5. To hold the ring of flowers to the edge of the basket, start at the base of the handle on the right hand side and bind the flowers to the basket with fine brass wire, threading it through the basket weave. See diagram 3.
6. Bind the handle with ribbon and add a bow and streamers to one side.
7. To finish off, add the rose petals.

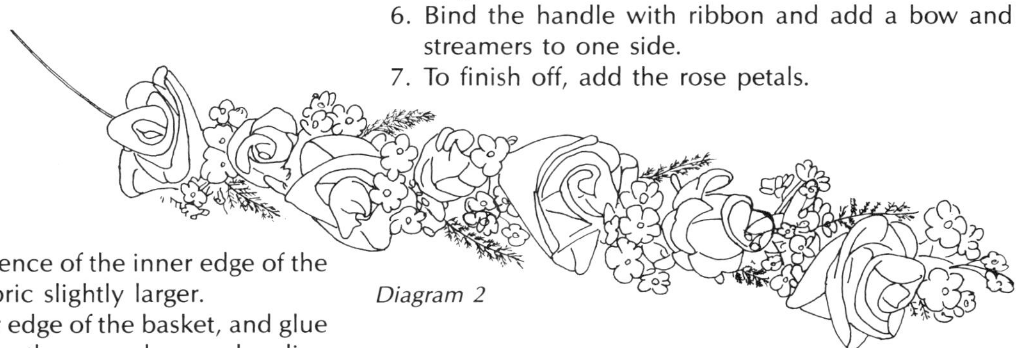

Diagram 2

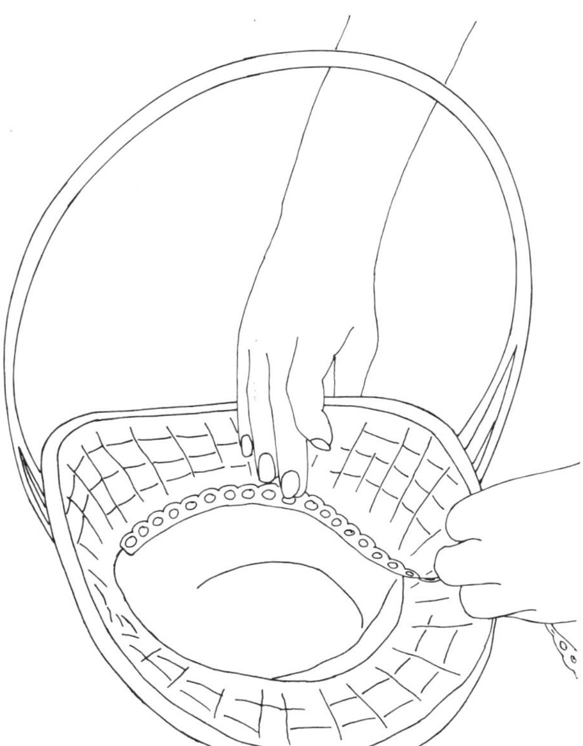

Diagram 1

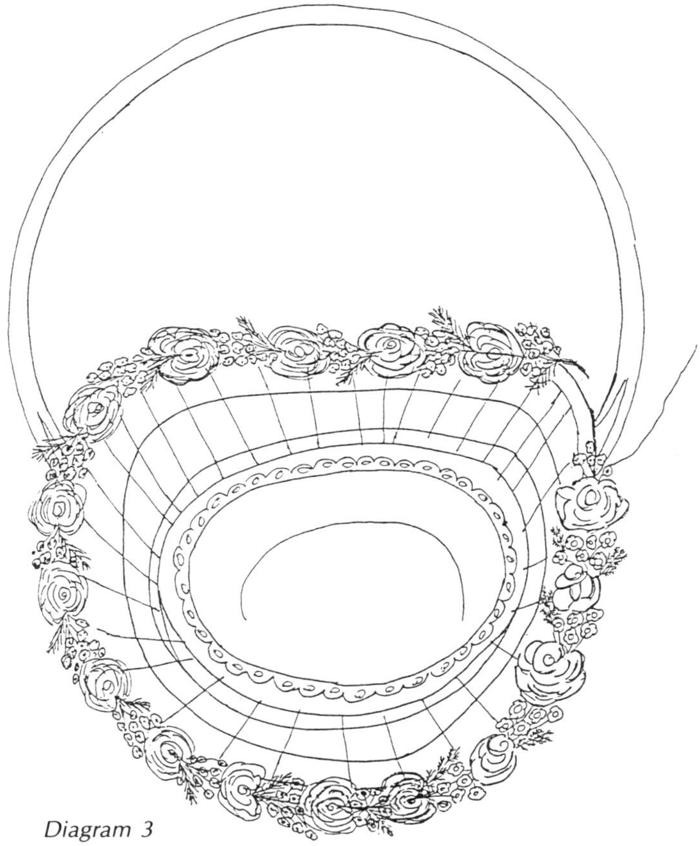

Diagram 3

Headwear for brides and bridesmaids

Equipment

Millinery wire
Scissors
Clear craft glue
Wire cutters
Tailor's chalk
32 gauge brass wire
White florist's tape
Thin metal headband
24 and 26 gauge florist's wire
Needle and cotton

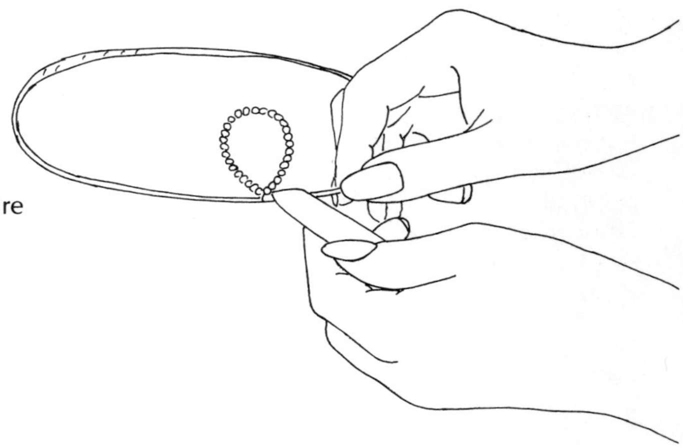

Diagram 1

Pearl loop tiara

Materials
60 cm (24'') millinery wire
white florist's tape
needle and cotton
clear craft glue
25 wire pearl loops
25 small drop pearls
50 seed pearls
1 m (39'') straw ribbon or tulle
60 cm (24'') half pearls
fine paper covered wire
comb

Method

1. Bend the millinery wire into a circle of the right head size or slightly smaller, overlapping the ends 5 cm (2'') and taping them together.
2. Remove the paper and untwist the wire of all pearl loops except one.
3. Tape a pearl loop to the wire circle. See diagram 1. Thread the next pearl loop through the previous loop, tape it to the wire circle, continuing thus right around the circle. See diagrams 2 and 3.

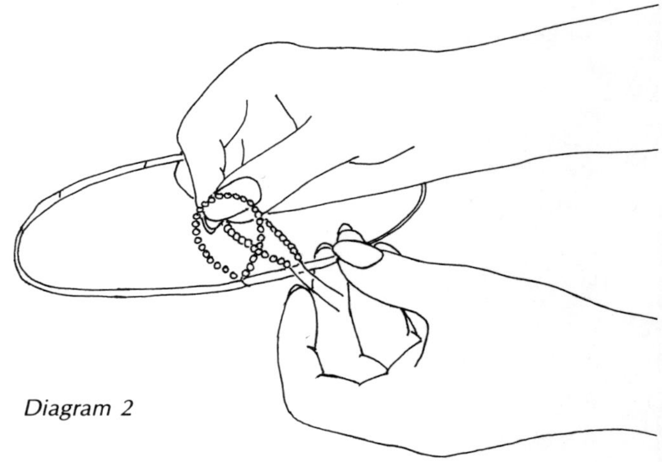

Diagram 2

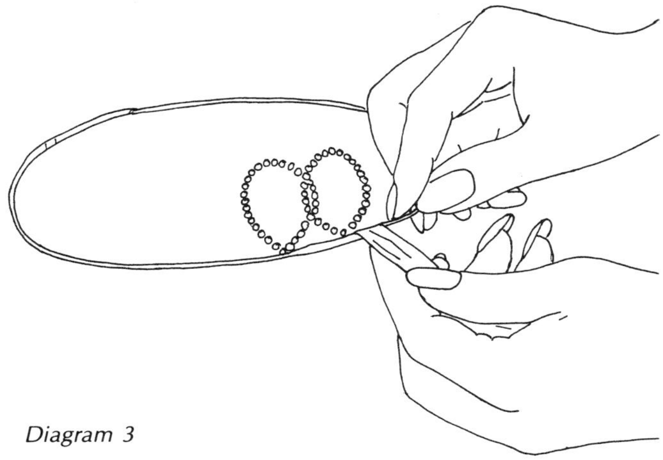

Diagram 3

4. To make the pearl drops, thread a seed pearl first, then the drop pearl and another seed pearl, then with the needle and cotton go back through the drop pearl and the first seed pearl. See diagram 4.

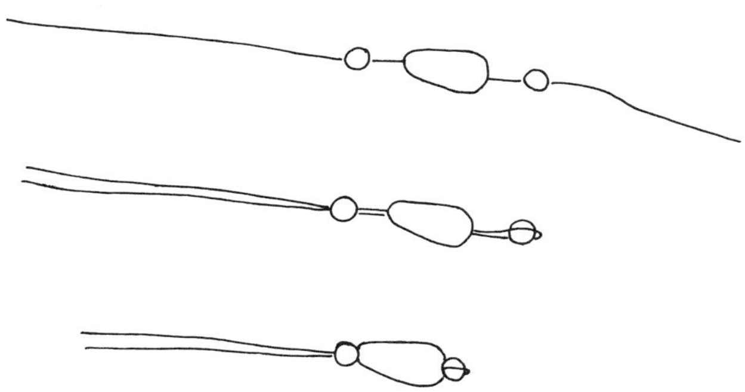

Diagram 4

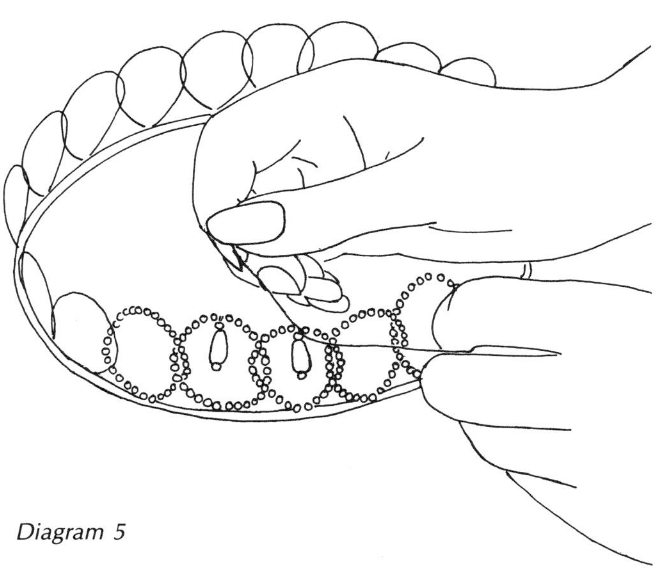

Diagram 5

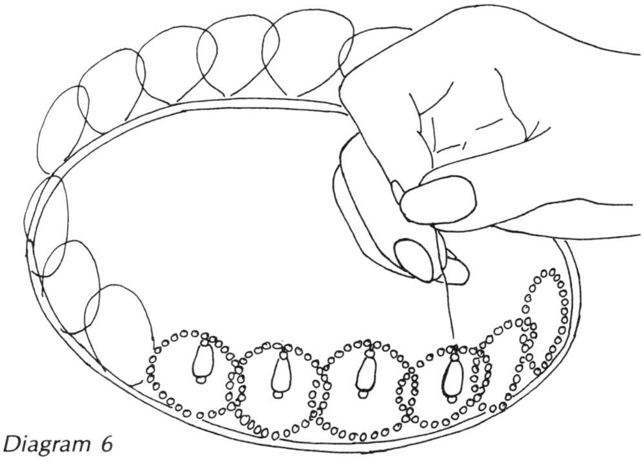

Diagram 6

5. Tie a pearl drop in the centre of each pearl loop with a double knot, cutting off excess cotton as closely as possible. Apply a small amount of glue with the point of a needle to each pearl drop. See diagrams 5 and 6.
6. Make two wire loops from the fine paper covered wire and tape them to the sides of the headpiece. See diagram 7.

(Continued on next page)

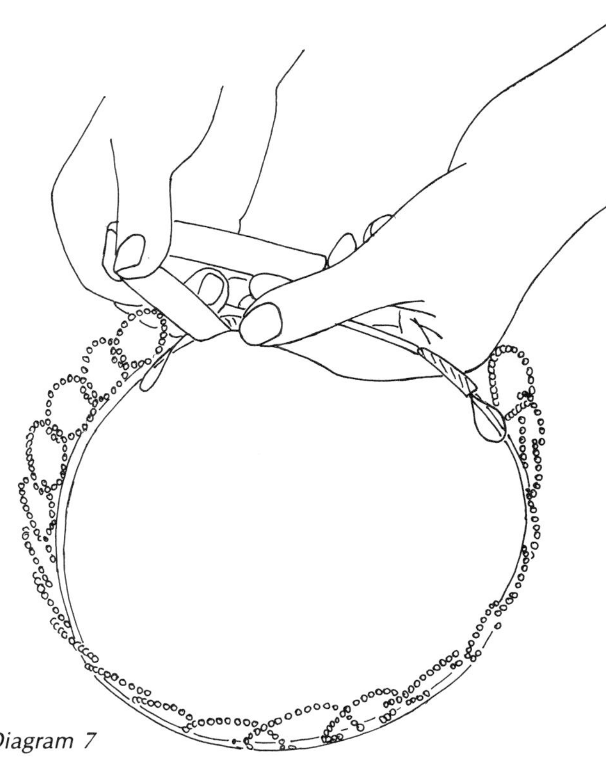

Diagram 7

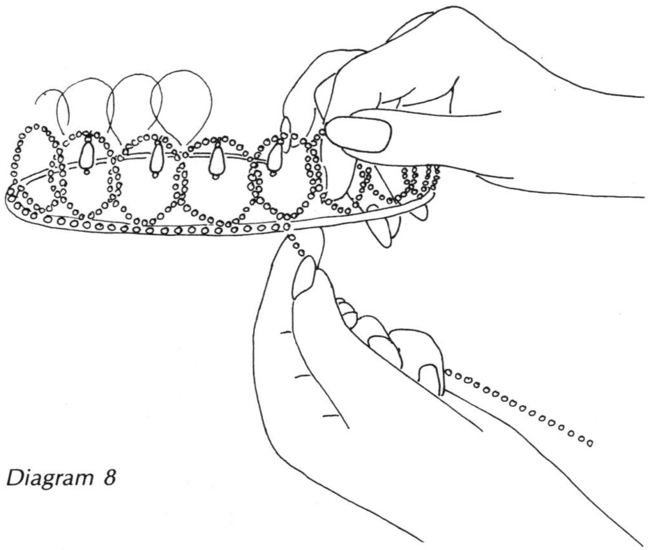

Diagram 8

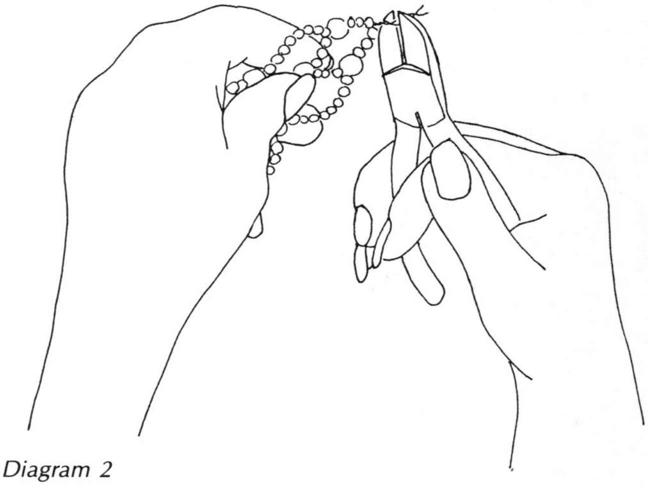

Diagram 2

7. To finish the tiara, bind the headpiece with straw ribbon or tulle, and glue a string of half pearls to the binding. See diagram 8.
8. Attach a comb to the back of the tiara with fine paper covered wire. Sew veil to the tiara if desired.

Plaited pearl tiara

Materials

1 plaited pearl headpiece
1 thin metal head band
3 medium pearl drops
4 small pearl drops
7 gold seed pearls
32 gauge brass wire
comb

Method

1. Remove the wire band from the plaited headpiece. See diagram 1.

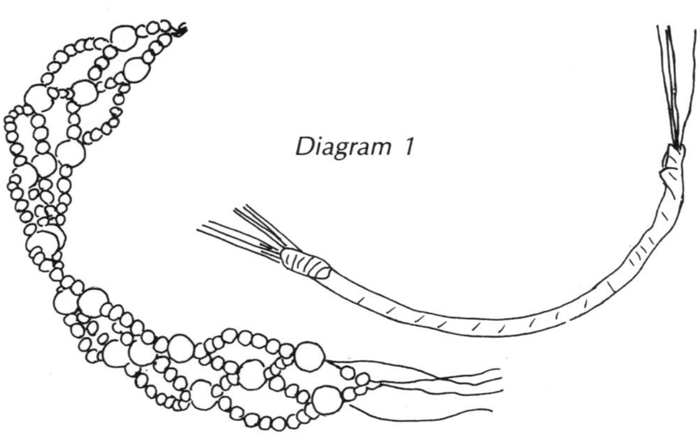

Diagram 1

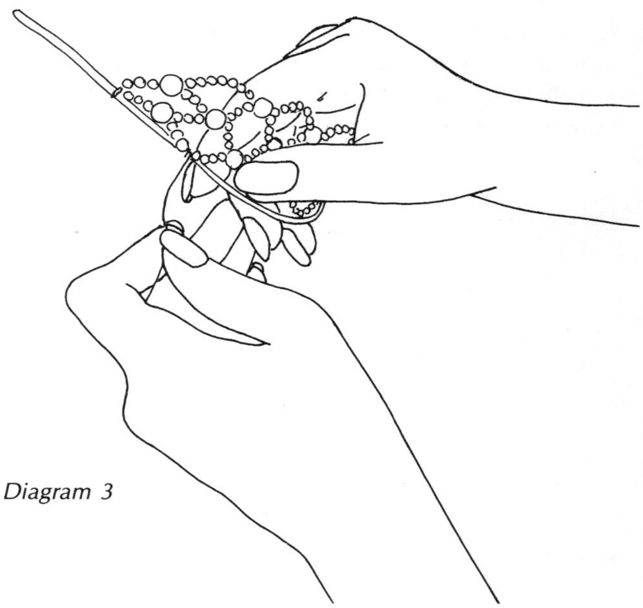

Diagram 3

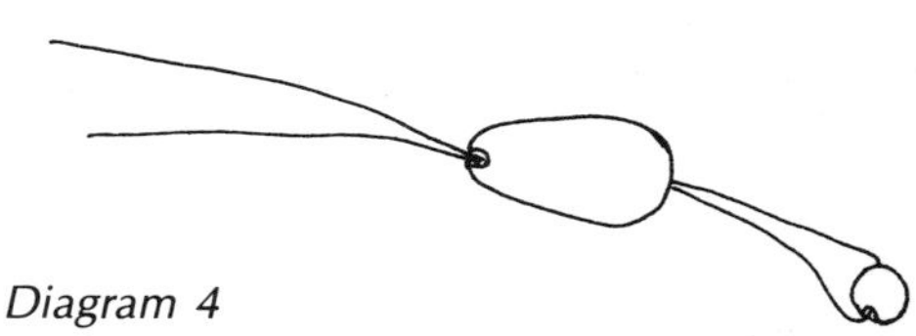

Diagram 4

2. Shorten the headpiece by removing some of the small pearls and the first large pearls at each end. Tidy up the ends by twisting the wires together and tucking them behind the pearls. See diagram 2.
3. Attach the pearl plait to the metal headband with 32 gauge brass wire. See diagram 3.
4. Now attach the pearl drops to the tiara. First thread one gold seed pearl onto 20 cm (8″) of brass wire, make a hairpin hook and thread this down through the pearl drop. See diagram 4.

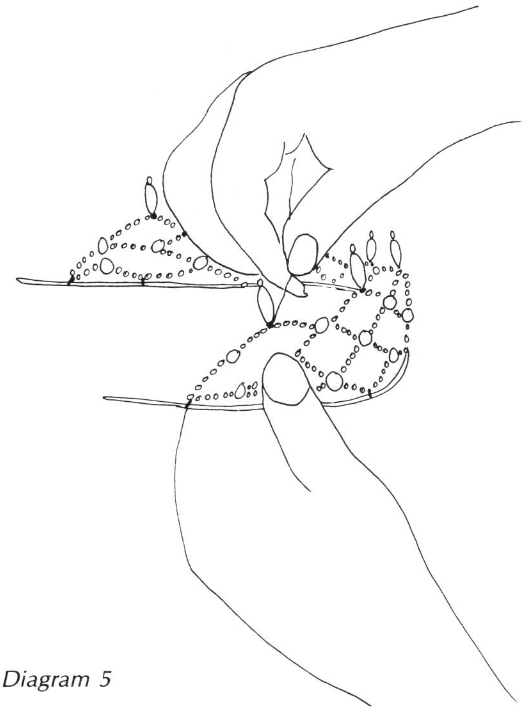

Diagram 5

5. Keeping the pearl drops rigid, twist the wire around the bottom of each one about four or five times in a figure eight pattern, then finish off by tucking the wire away at the back of the headpiece. See diagram 5. Use the three medium pearls at centre front of the headpiece, with two small ones either side.
6. Attach a comb to the inside of the tiara with fine brass wire. See diagram 6.

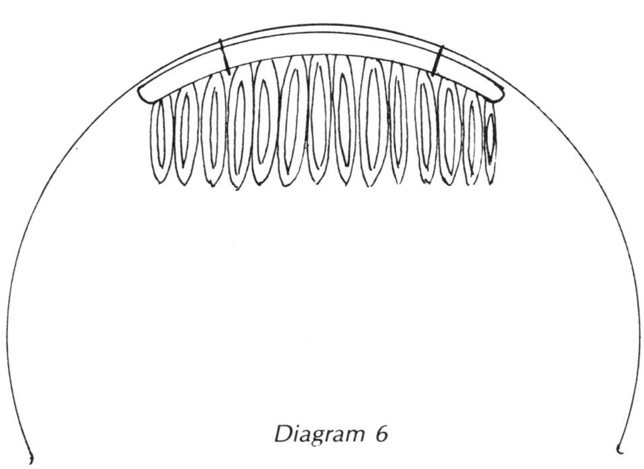

Diagram 6

Satin bridal band

Materials
1 plastic Alice band
30 cm x 6 cm (12″ x 2½″) sponge or wadding
5 cm x 16 cm (2″ x 6½″) satin fabric
40 cm x 1 cm (16″ x 3/8″) lace
clear craft glue
comb

Method

1. Cut the satin on the cross or bias 1 cm (3/8″) larger than the Alice band, tapering the fabric slightly at the ends.
2. Apply glue to the top of the band and glue the wadding down. Trim away excess wadding.
3. Apply glue to the underside of the band, and place the satin over the band, stretching it at the same time and gluing the ends down first. See diagrams 1 and 2.

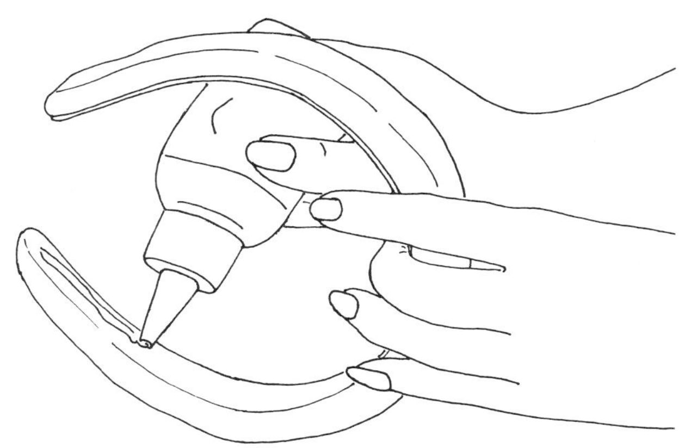

Diagram 1

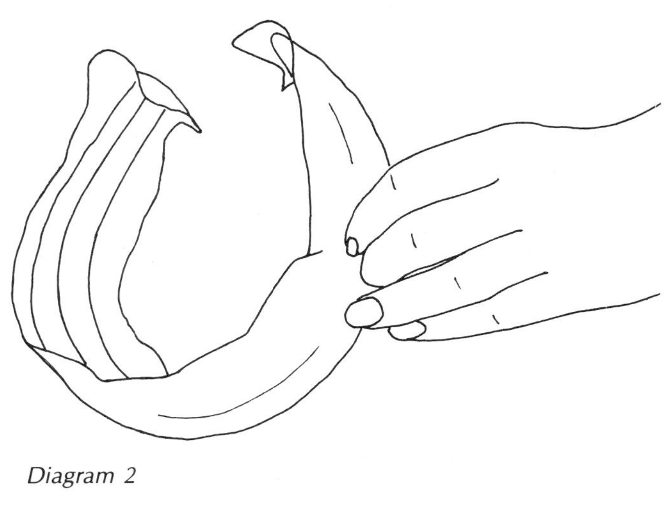

Diagram 2

Lace and satin tiara

Materials

40 cm (16″) buckram or Leno
1.5 m (1¼″ yds) millinery wire
50 cm x 7 cm (20″ x 3″) scalloped lace
pearls and sequins
60 cm x 20 cm (25″ x 8″) satin fabric
clear craft glue
white florist's tape
comb

Method

1. Pin the lace to the buckram, outline the top of the lace with tailor's chalk or pencil and remove. Cut the buckram along the outline of the lace. See diagrams 1 and 2.

Diagram 1

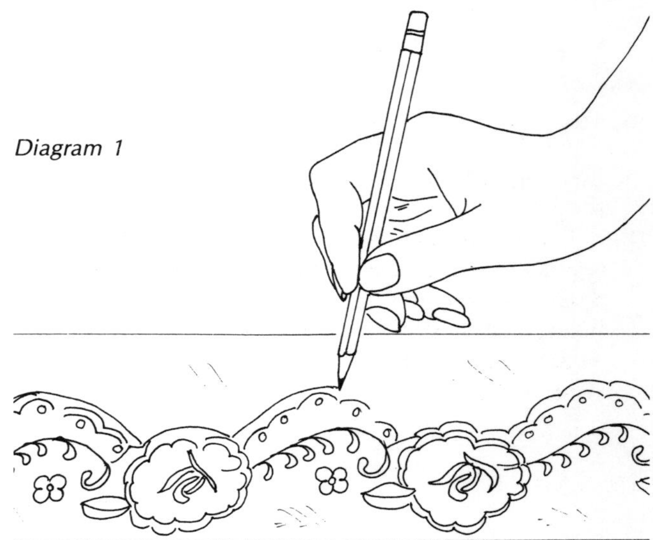

Diagram 2

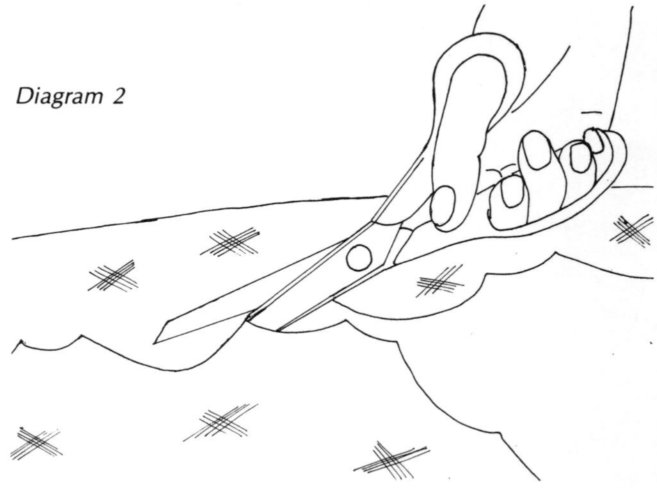

Diagram 3

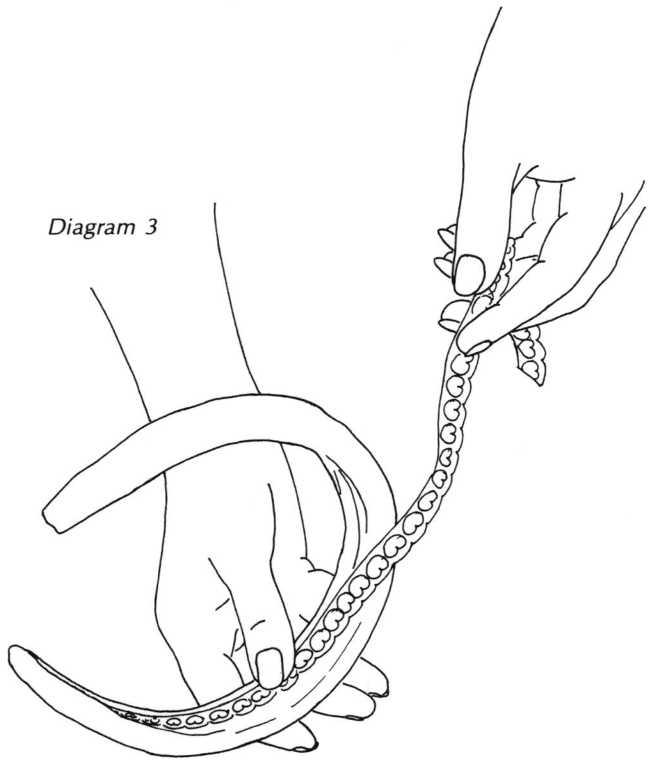

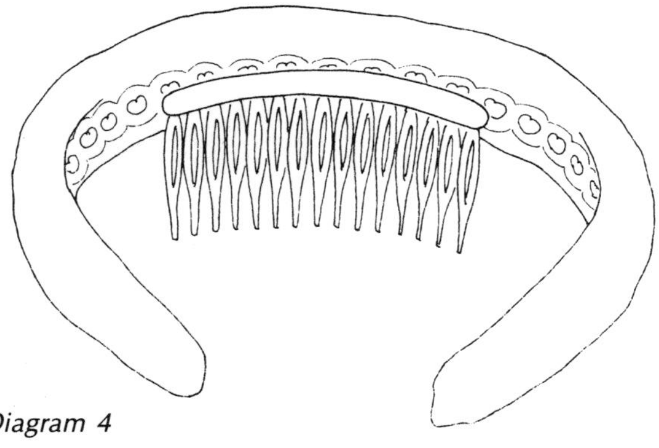

Diagram 4

4. Fold and glue the rest of the fabric under the band.
5. To finish off the headband apply glue to the underside of the band down the centre and glue the lace down. See diagram 3.
6. To affix the comb to the band, apply a bead of glue on the top of the comb and press in place at the back of the band. See diagram 4.

2. Wire around the top and bottom edges of the buckram, either with buttonhole stitch or machine zig-zag. Tape the ends of the wires together, extending the wire 10 cm (4'') each side of the headpiece. See diagram 3.
3. Apply glue to the top front edge of the buckram. Position the satin behind the buckram and bring it over the front top edge, trimming and clipping the edge of the satin to match the scallops and eliminate bulk. Glue down. See diagram 4.
4. Apply more glue to the top front edge, bring the satin up and glue in place, cutting away excess fabric as close as you can to the top edge. See diagram 5.
5. Apply glue to the top and bottom edges of the lace and glue to the front of the tiara.
6. To tidy the back of the tiara, overlap the wires 5 cm (2'') at the right head measurement, cut off any excess and tape together, then bind with tulle.
7. Lastly glue sequins and pearls over the lace if desired.

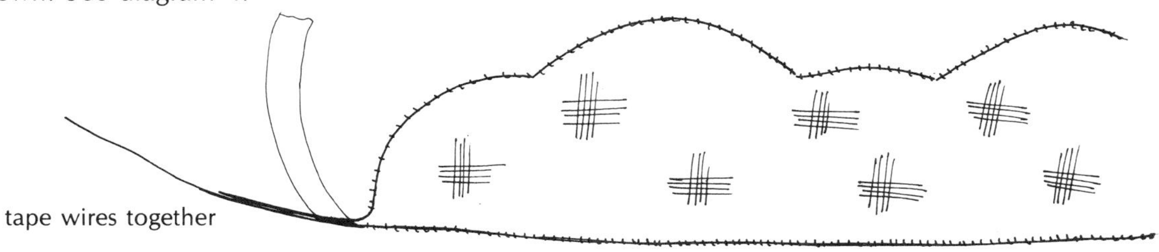

Diagram 3

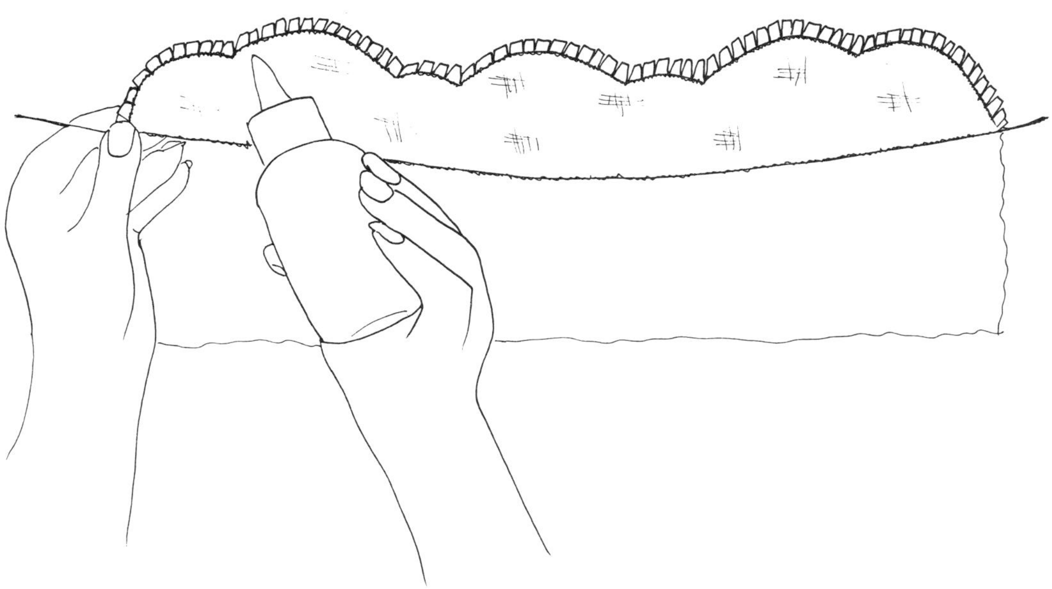

Diagram 4

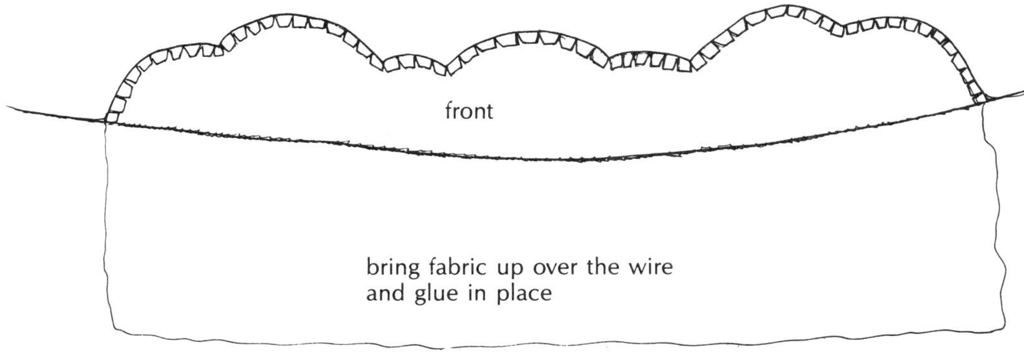

Diagram 5

Traditional floral headpiece

Materials
6 medium cream roses
17 mini pink roses
17 wired gum leaves
dried baby's breath
florist's tape
25 cm (10'') millinery wire
comb

Method
1. Tape each mini rose with a small bunch of baby's breath.
2. Starting at one end, tape to the millinery wire one gum leaf and one mini rose, then two gum leaves either side of the wire, one medium rose, three mini roses, one medium rose and two gum leaves. See diagram.
3. Continue this pattern until you reach the middle of the headpiece.
4. Starting at the opposite end, repeat the above pattern until you reach the centre again.
5. To finish off headpiece attach a comb at the centre.

Handmade rose headpiece

Materials
6 handmade rosebuds
10 small to medium handmade roses
23 handmade fabric leaves
2 bunches pearl loops
1 bunch pearl stamens
1 bunch pearl sprays
white florist's tape
20 cm (8'') millinery wire
24 gauge wire
comb

Method
1. Make 6 rosebuds, 10 medium size roses and 23 fabric leaves following the instructions on pages 59 and 61.
2. Take three stamens, fold in half. Place a piece of florist's wire against them and tape together. Make three of these bundles.
3. Now make a three-petalled flower out of fabric leaves by taping three leaves together with a pearl stamen bundle in the centre. Make three of these flowers. See diagram 1.

Diagram 1

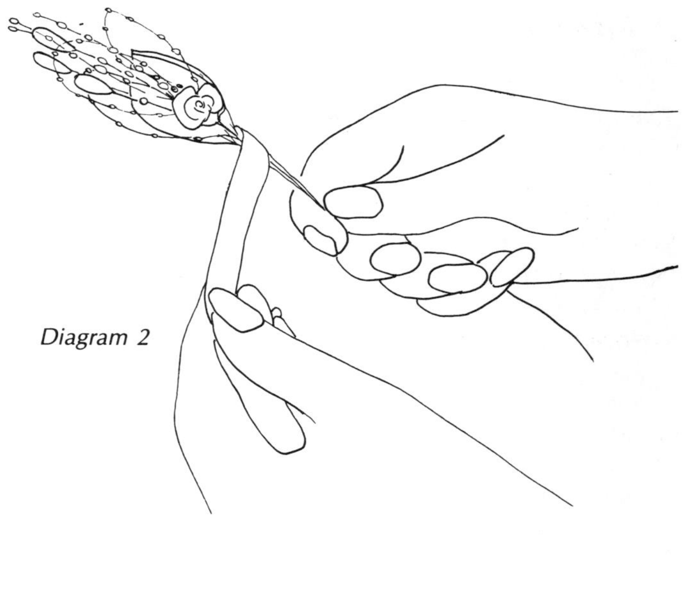

Diagram 2

4. Before starting the headpiece tape a bunch of pearl loops to each of the remaining 14 fabric leaves.
5. Now tape one bunch of pearl sprays and one rosebud to two of the leaves and tape them to either end of the millinery wire. See diagrams 2 and 3.
6. Add two rosebuds in line at either end as shown in diagram 4.
7. Now tape the remaining fabric leaves and the roses down each side of the millinery wire, following the pattern in diagram 4.
8. Tape the fabric flowers in the middle of the headpiece at points 1, 2 and 3.
9. Finish off headpiece by adding comb.

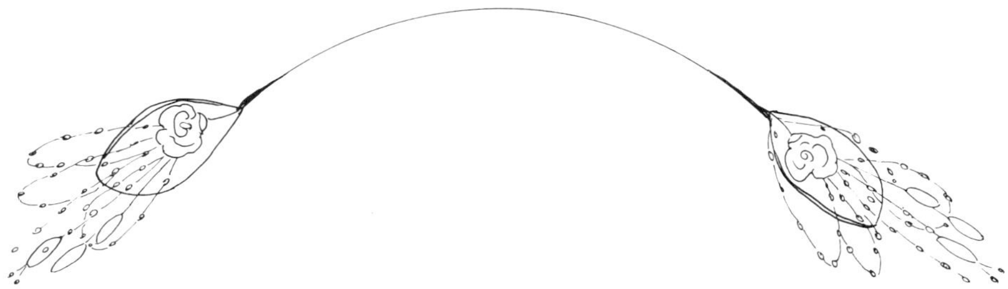

Diagram 3

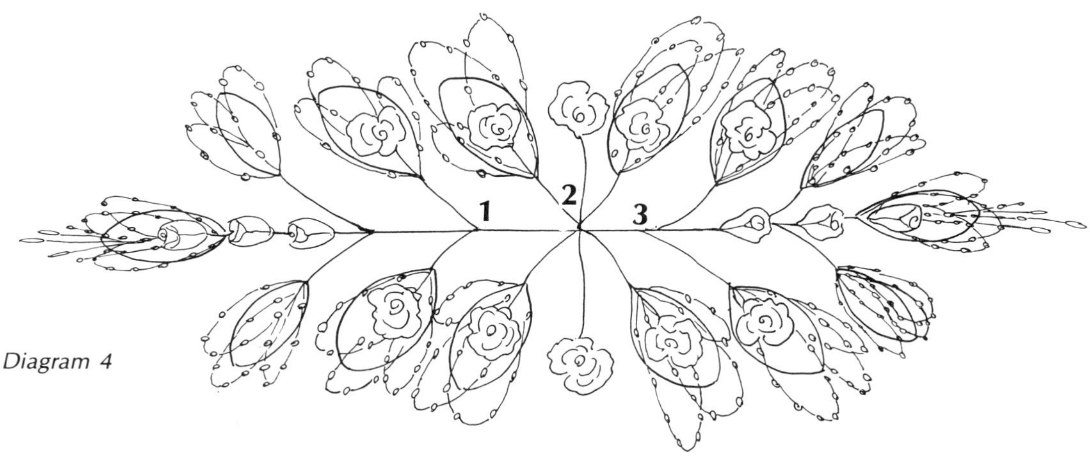

Diagram 4

Bridal circlet

Materials

9 white ribbon roses
9 white azaleas or similar flowers
18 small white satin or millinery leaves
18 white mini roses
1 bunch pearl loops
60 cm (24″) millinery wire
white florist's tape
comb

Method

1. Make 9 ribbon roses and 18 satin leaves following the instructions on pages 60 and 61.
2. Bend the millinery wire into a circle of the right head size, overlapping the ends 5 cm (2″) and taping them together.
3. Tape three pearl loops to each azalea and cut off all stems to about 4 cm (1½″).
4. Starting at the back, tape *1*, one ribbon rose; *2*, one mini rose; *3*, one leaf; *4*, one azalea; *5*, one leaf; *6*, one mini rose, continuing this zig-zag sequence to the end. See diagram 1 over the page.
5. Finish off by attaching the comb, tying it to the back of the circlet with fine covered wire. See diagram 2 on the next page.

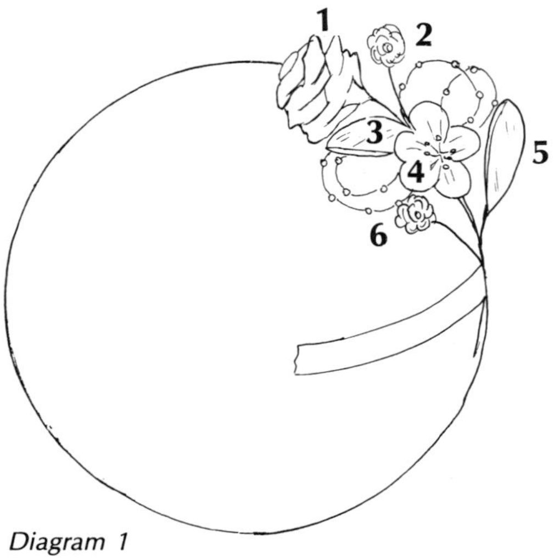

Diagram 1

Diagram 2

Bridesmaid's circlet

Materials
8 apricot roses
8 cream roses
1 bunch forget-me-nots
dried baby's breath
60 cm (24'') millinery wire
white florist's tape

Method
1. Bend the millinery wire into a circle of the right head size, overlapping the ends 5 cm (2'').
2. Starting at the back, tape the flowers to the wire in the following order: *1*, apricot rose; *2*, baby's breath; *3*, cream rose; *4*, baby's breath; *5*, forget-me-nots. Continue this sequence until the end. See diagram.
3. Finish off with comb.

Flowergirl's headband

Materials
1 plastic Alice band
3 pink roses
4 cream roses
12 gum leaves
dried baby's breath
craft glue or glue gun
comb (optional)

Method
1. Remove all stems from the artificial flowers and trim away any stems left on the gum leaves.
2. Apply glue all over the top of the band and glue leaves in place, starting at the ends and working in to the middle. See diagram 1.
3. Glue each flower to the band over the leaves, spacing them evenly, and leaving about 5 cm (2″) at each end of the band. See diagram 2.
4. Add the baby's breath in small bunches, applying a liberal amount of glue to the stems and placing them in and around the roses. See diagram 3.
5. To finish off, glue a comb to the back of the headband.

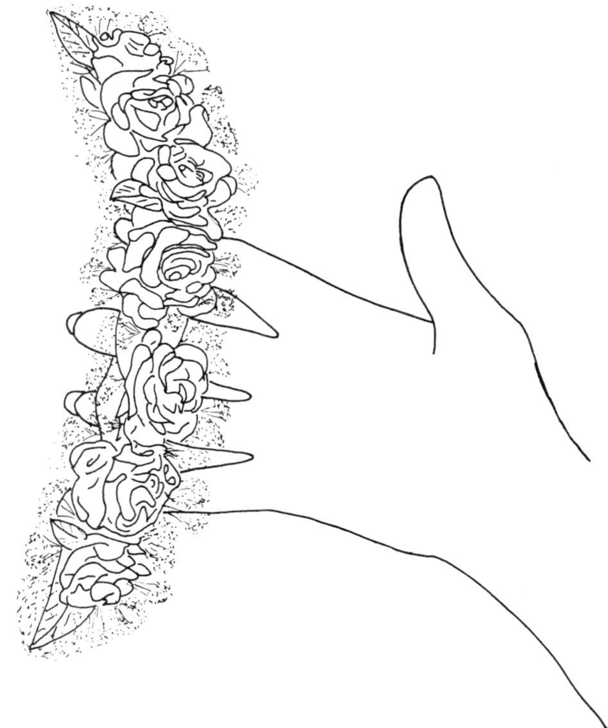

Diagram 2

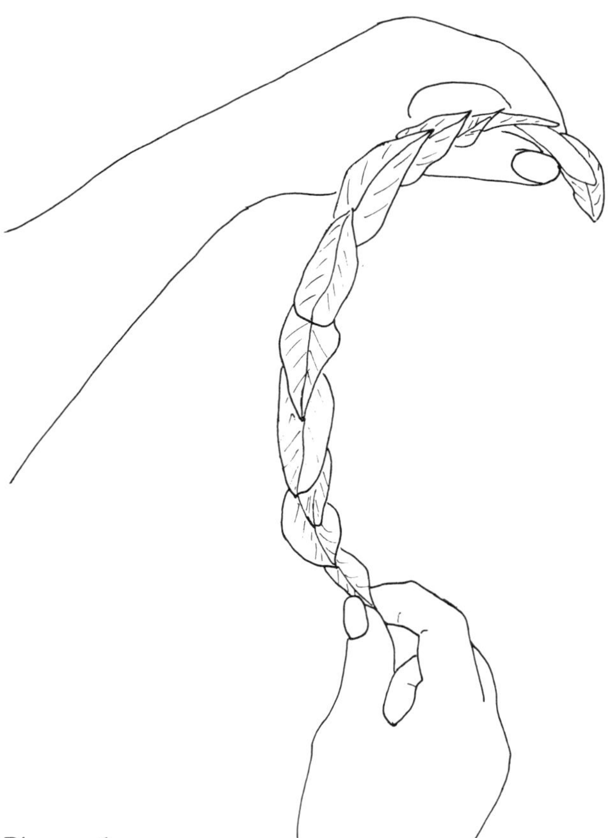

Diagram 1

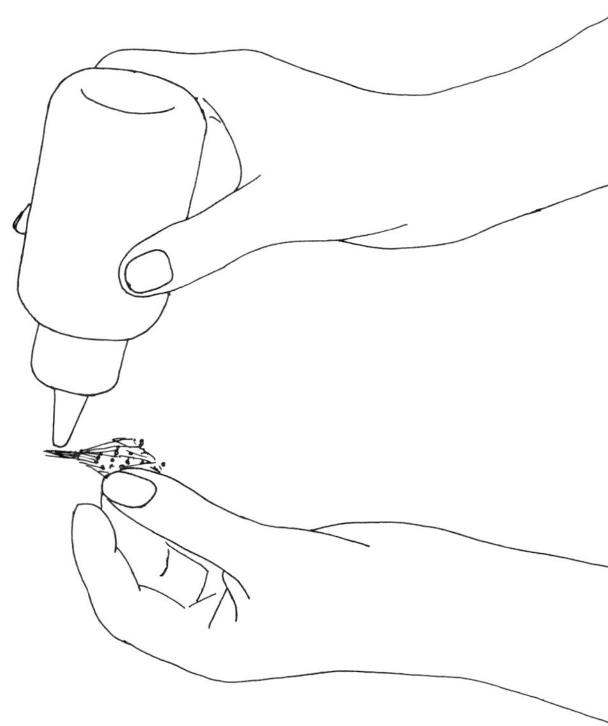

Diagram 3

Flowergirl's side comb

Materials
3 pink flowers
baby's breath
3 or 4 gum leaves
clear craft glue
comb

Method
1. Follow the instructions for the flowergirl band, trimming the stems and gluing the leaves to the comb first. See diagram 1.
2. Glue the three flowers in place, and finish off the comb with baby's breath. See diagram 2.

Diagram 1

Diagram 2

Wedding party accessories

Rose and ivy corsage

Materials
5 apricot roses
1 stem bell flowers
1 three-leaf ivy stem
2 single ivy leaves
50 cm x 10 mm (20 x ¼″) apricot ribbon
26 and 24 gauge wire
green florist's tape

Method
1. Wire all roses if needed, following the instructions on pages 7–13.
2. Lay one rose and one bunch of bell flowers against the three-leaf ivy stem and tape them together. See diagram 1.

Diagram 1

3. Tape the next three roses, laying one rose each side of the first rose with the third in the centre, adding one bunch of bell flowers.
4. Tape the two ivy leaves either side of the last three roses, then tape the last rose to the left, as shown in diagram 2.
5. To finish off the corsage make a four-loop bow (see page 52) and tape it to the right-hand side of the corsage. Cut off excess wire to 3 cm (1½″) and bind with more florist's tape.

Diagram 2

Rose and fern corsage

Materials
3 fern leaves
5 small cream roses
50 cm x 10 mm (20″ x ¼″) cream satin ribbon
26 and 24 gauge wire
green florist's tape

Method
1. Wire all roses if necessary (see pages 7–13).
2. Lay one rose against one fern stem, fairly close to the top of the fern, and tape together. See diagram 1.

Diagram 1

Diagram 2

3. Take the other two fern stems and tape them about 5 cm (2″) below the rose. See diagram 2.
4. Tape two roses either side of the first rose, the fourth rose in the centre and the fifth rose on the left. See diagram 3.
5. To finish off the corsage make a four-loop bow (see page 60) and tape it to the right hand side of the corsage. Cut off excess wire to 3 cm (1½″) and bind with more florist's tape.

Diagram 3

Carnation buttonhole

Materials
1 three-leaf ivy stem
1 carnation
green florist's tape
dried baby's breath

Method
1. You can use the original carnation stem in this instance, applying glue to one end of the artificial stem and inserting it back into the flower head.
2. Cut ivy and carnation stems to about 5 cm (2''). Lay the carnation against the ivy leaf and tape together. See diagram 1.
3. Place a small amount of baby's breath just below the carnation and tape together. You can wire the baby's breath first if you like, but the florist's tape will hold it quite securely without wiring. See diagram 2.

Diagram 1

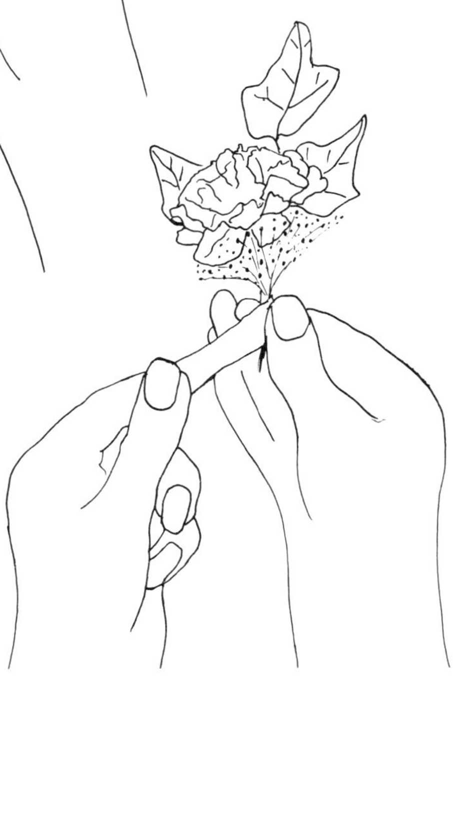

Diagram 2

Rose buttonhole

Materials
2 fern leaves
1 rose
green florist's tape
dried baby's breath

Method
1. Keeping the original rose stem, cut the fern and rose stems to about 5 cm (2'').
2. Take the two fern stems and lay them together, one just below the other, and tape together. Lay the rose against the fern and tape together. See diagram.
3. Place a small amount of baby's breath just below the rose and bind with florist's tape.

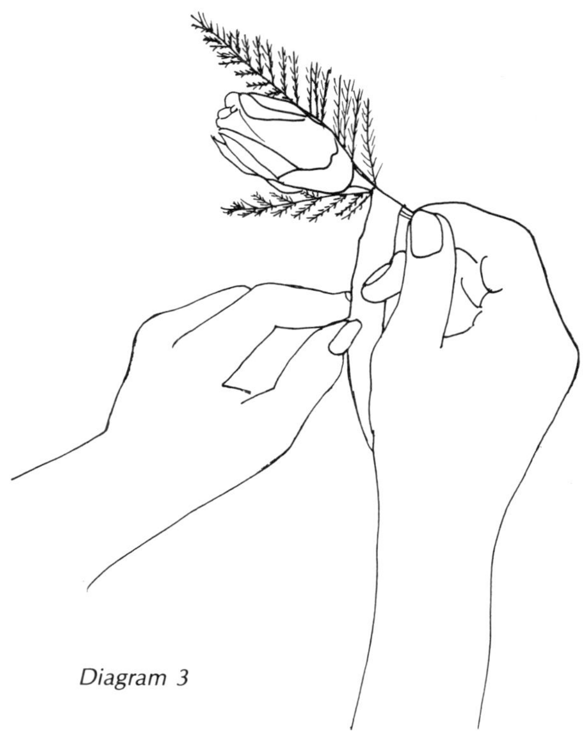

Diagram 3

Ceremony and reception

Flower and tulle pew decoration

Materials
6 rosebuds (or one large rose)
5 tulle or net tufts
5 m x 10 mm (5½ yds x ½'') satin ribbon
24 gauge florist's wire
white florist's tape

Method
1. Make five net tufts following the instructions given on page 62.
2. Wire flowers if necessary, following the instructions on pages 7–13.
3. If you are using rosebuds, arrange them like a posy and tape together. Place the tulle tufts around the rosebuds or the single rose and tape together. See diagram 1.
4. Make ribbon streamers and tape them to the posy. Cut away excess wire to a length of 6 cm (2½'').
5. Tidy the wire handle, bind with more florist's tape and bend it down to make tying the decoration to the pew easier. See diagram 2.

Diagram 1

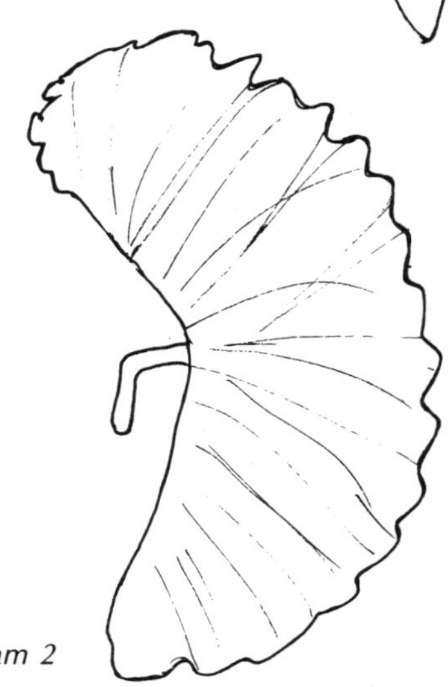

Diagram 2

Elegant and simple satin bridal band can be worn with either a short or long veil (page 29)

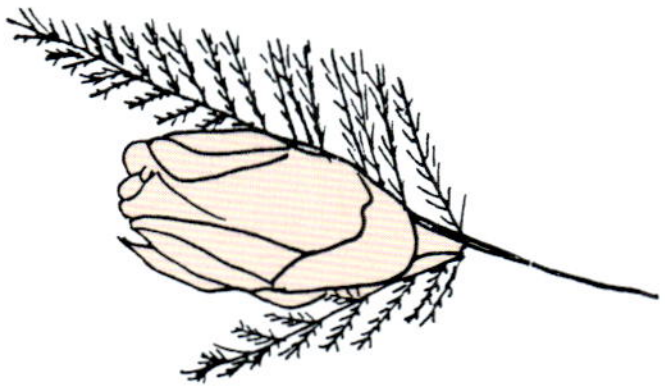

This stunning tiara of lace and satin anchors a lovely finger-tip veil (page 30)

Traditional floral headpiece combines medium cream roses, pink mini roses, gum leaves and dried baby's breath (page 32)

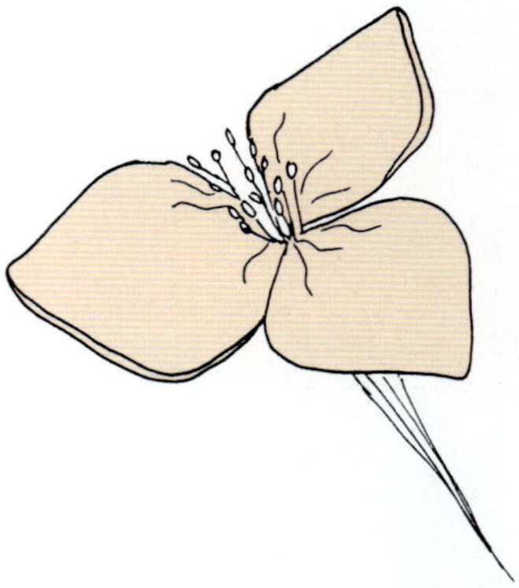

Handmade rose headpiece contains roses, rosebuds and leaves to stunning effect (page 32)

A bridal circlet of ribbon roses, azaleas, mini roses and satin leaves set off by pearl loops (page 33)

Dainty bridesmaid's circlet of cream and apricot roses, forget-me-nots and baby's breath (page 34)

Pew bow

Materials

1 roll white or cream paper ribbon
fine paper-covered wire
25 cm x 5 mm (10″ x ¼″) white satin ribbon

Method

1. Cut paper ribbon into three 60 cm (24″) lengths. Fold the ends of one paper strip into the centre, overlapping slightly. Do the same with the second length of paper, making the bow slightly smaller.
3. Place the smaller bow on top of the larger one and secure with fine wire. See diagram 1.
4. Wrap the third length of paper ribbon around the centre of the bow and secure with fine paper-covered wire. See diagrams 2 and 3.
5. Thread the satin ribbon through the back of the bow to tie the decoration to the pew. See diagram 4.

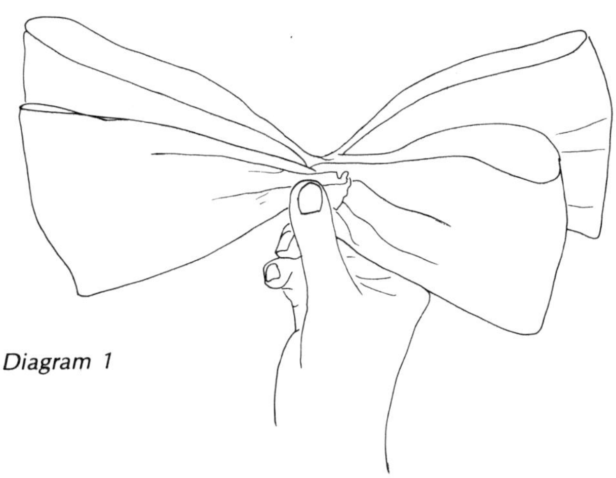

Diagram 1

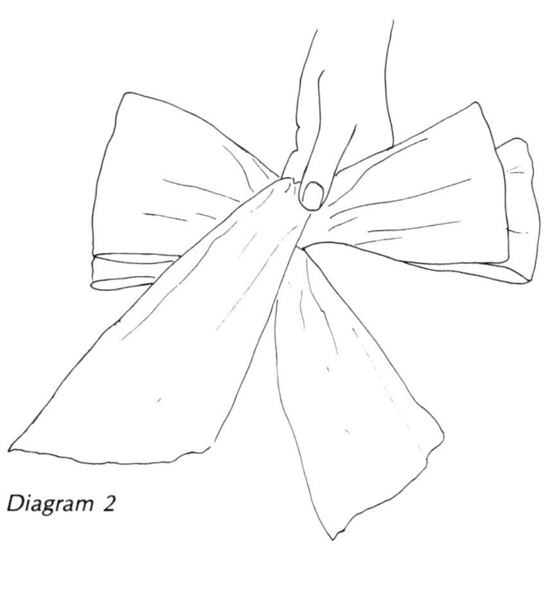

Diagram 2

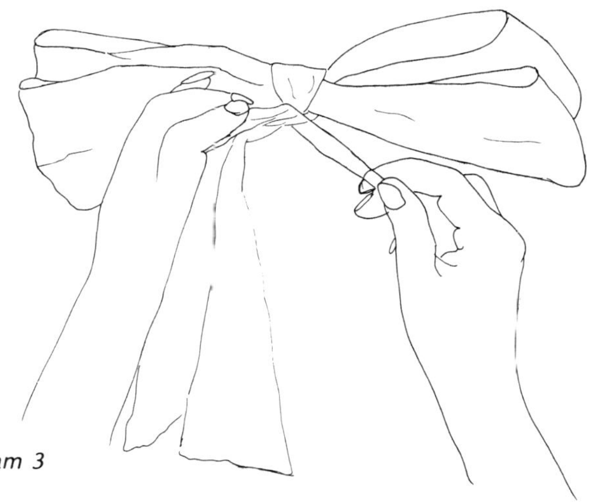

Diagram 3

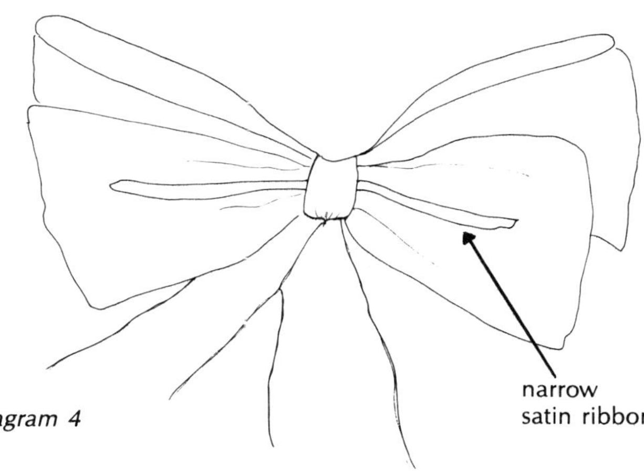

Diagram 4

Tulle topiary tree

Materials

1 wooden dowel 100 cm x 3 cm (39″ x 1½″)
1 cream or white plastic pot (or painted terracotta pot)
white paint
plaster of Paris
5 m (5½ yds) white net
3 m (3½ yds) satin ribbon
20 white roses
22 gauge florist's wire
large Oasis ball
white florist's tape

Method

1. Make twelve large net tufts following the instructions on page 62.

2. Paint the wooden dowel white. Line the pot with plastic or other material to block the holes. Prepare the plaster of Paris following the instructions on the packet and pour into pot, push the dowel into the wet plaster and secure the dowel upright until the plaster is completely set.
3. Push the Oasis ball onto the dowel, being careful not to press too hard.
4. Tape the rose stems with white florist's tape and cut to about 20 cm (8''). Position them evenly around the Oasis ball. See diagram 1.
5. Position the net tufts in between the roses. Make a long three-loop ribbon streamer and push it into the Oasis just under the net at the front of the topiary tree. See diagram 2.
6. To finish the decoration make three or four small net tufts and glue them to the top of the plaster.

Diagram 1

Diagram 2

Wedding cake top

Materials
13 apricot mini rosebuds
6 white mini rosebuds
12 bunches white forget-me-nots
6 bunches apricot forget-me-nots
white florist's tape
26 gauge wire
6 x 3 mm (3/8'') wide ribbon bows

Method
1. Wire the flowers if necessary. Make six small ribbon bows following the instructions on pages 52 and 57.
2. This decoration follows the same principles as the traditional posy, only on a smaller scale. Place six white rosebuds and six apricot forget-me-nots evenly around one apricot rosebud and tape together. See diagram 1.
3. In the second row, place six ribbon bows below the white rosebuds and tape together. In the last row, tape together twelve apricot rosebuds with twelve bunches of white forget-me-nots in between. See diagram 2.
4. Tidy up the cake top posy by cutting away excess wire and retaping.
5. Check the state of the icing before fixing the cake top to the cake. If the icing has set fairly hard, cut a small hole with a sharp knife before pushing the posy into the cake.

Diagram 1

Diagram 2

Cake spray

Materials
1 apricot mini rose
5 white mini roses
6 bunches apricot forget-me-nots
1 bunch white forget-me-nots
white florist's tape
26 gauge wire

Method
1. Make a mini posy, arranging the white rosebuds and the forget-me-nots around the apricot rosebuds, and tape together. See diagram 1.
2. To make a trail, dismantle two bunches of forget-me-nots — one apricot, one white. Tape seven individual forget-me-nots to a 26 gauge wire. See diagram 2.
3. Place the trail against the posy and tape together. See diagram 3.
4. When placing the spray on the cake, arrange the flowers so they are trailing down the side of the cake.

Diagram 3

Diagram 1

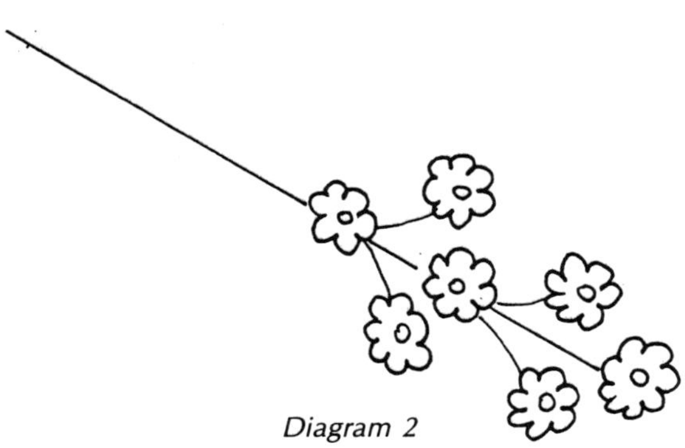

Diagram 2

Bridal table arrangement

Materials
20 large apricot rosebuds
8 large white or cream rosebuds
small block Oasis
small glass bowl (or paper doily)
1 candle
1 bunch of dried gum
dried baby's breath (optional)

Method
1. There should be no need to rewire the roses or dried gum as their original stems are fairly strong.
2. Place the Oasis in a glass bowl or glue it to a doily.
3. Cut the apricot rosebud stems to various lengths, the longer ones for the ends about 18 cm (7″), and the side ones about 12 cm (5″). Position them in the Oasis following diagram 1.
4. Cut the dried gum and white rosebud stems to various lengths and position them in and around the apricot rosebuds. See diagram 2.
5. You can keep adding gum or other flowers if necessary to fill in any gaps and to hide the Oasis.

Diagram 1

Diagram 2

Guest table centrepiece

Materials

1 medium size paper doily, white or gold
thick cardboard 25 cm x 25 cm (10″ x 10″) square
Oasis 8 cm x 8 cm (3½″ x 3½″) square
1 candle
clear craft glue
8 tulle or net tufts
22 gauge florist's wire
gold spray paint (optional)
7 rosebuds (optional)

Method

1. Spray the doily gold if necessary. Cut the cardboard slightly smaller than the doily, then apply glue to the cardboard and glue the doily on top.
2. Apply glue to the bottom of the Oasis and glue it on top of the doily. See diagram 1.
3. Make eight net tufts according to the instructions on page 62.
4. Push the candle into the centre of the Oasis, and surround closely with three net tufts pushed into the top of the Oasis.
5. Position the remaining net tufts to cover the Oasis. Cut the rosebud stems to about 10 cm (4″) and place them in between the net tufts. See diagram 2.

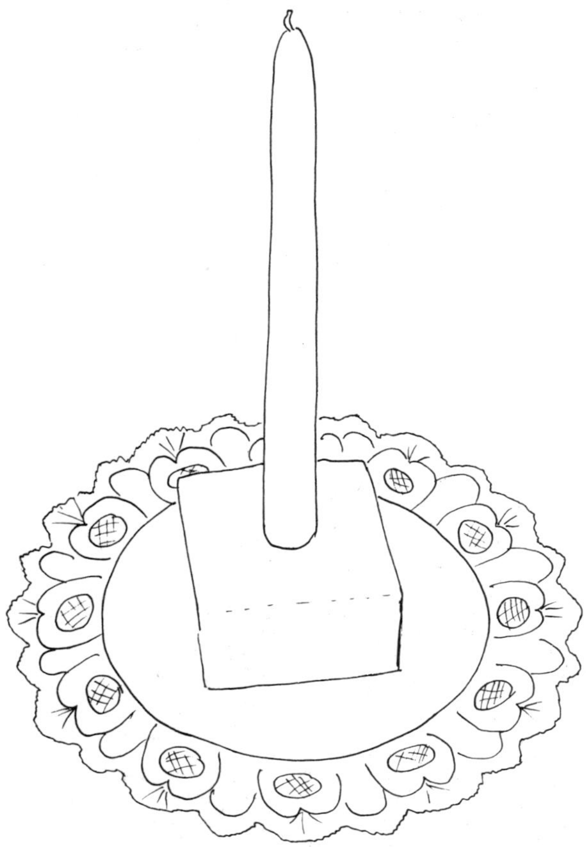

Diagram 1

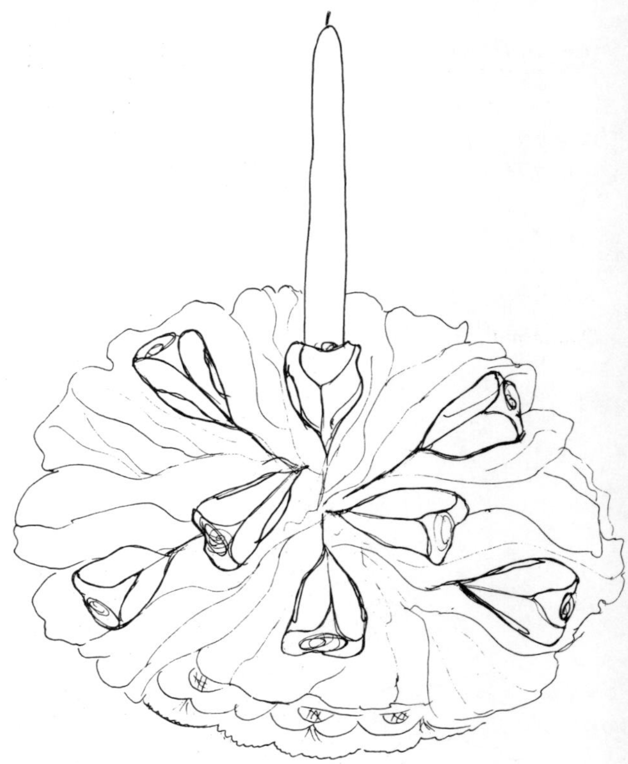

Diagram 2

Floral and headwear trims

Looped ribbon streamers

Materials
1.6 m x 2 cm (1¾ yds x 1″) ribbon
white or green florist's tape
22 gauge wire

Method

1. Cut the ribbon into three separate lengths of 70 cm (28″), 55 cm (22″) and 35 cm (14″). Gather the ends together, graduating from the shortest to the longest. See diagram 1.
2. Turn the ribbon over and place a 22 gauge wire with a hook at one end flat against the ribbon. Twist the wire around the end of the ribbon very tightly. See diagrams 2 and 3.
3. Tape the ends to hide the wire, continuing down the wire for about 10 cm (4″). See diagram 4 on the next page.

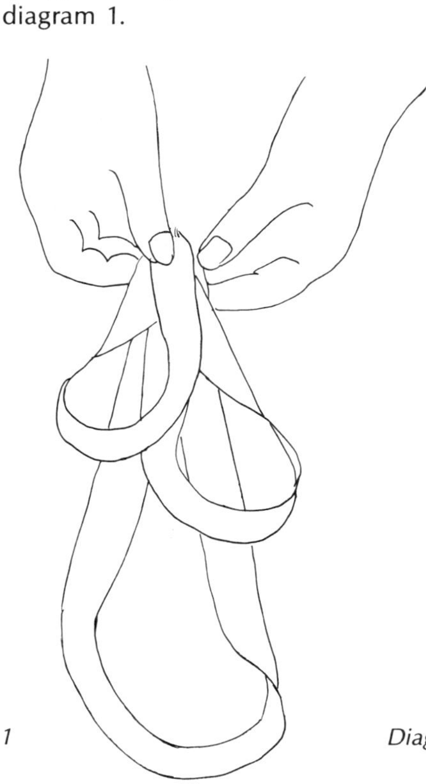

Diagram 1

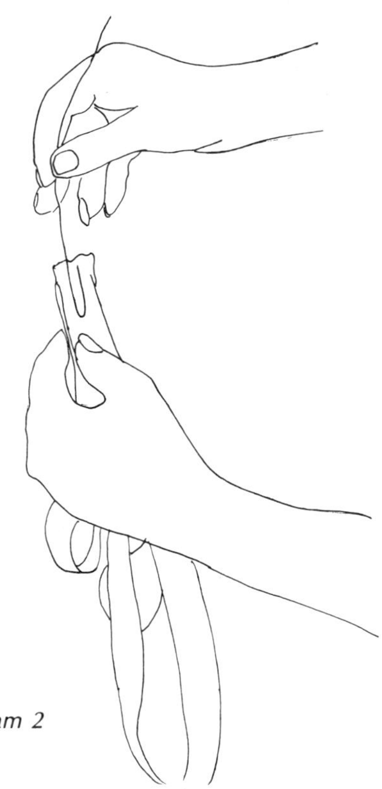

Diagram 2

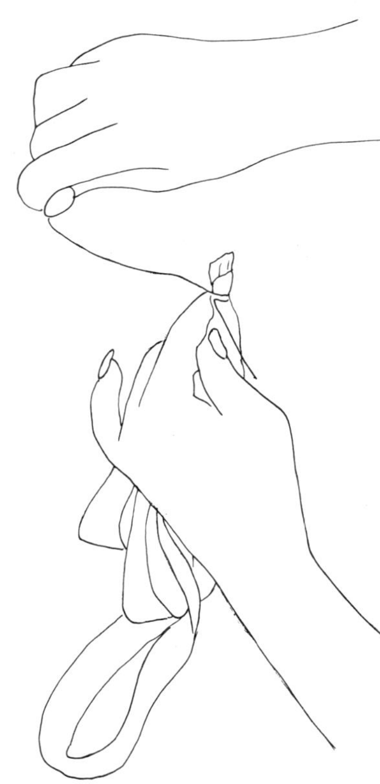

Diagram 3

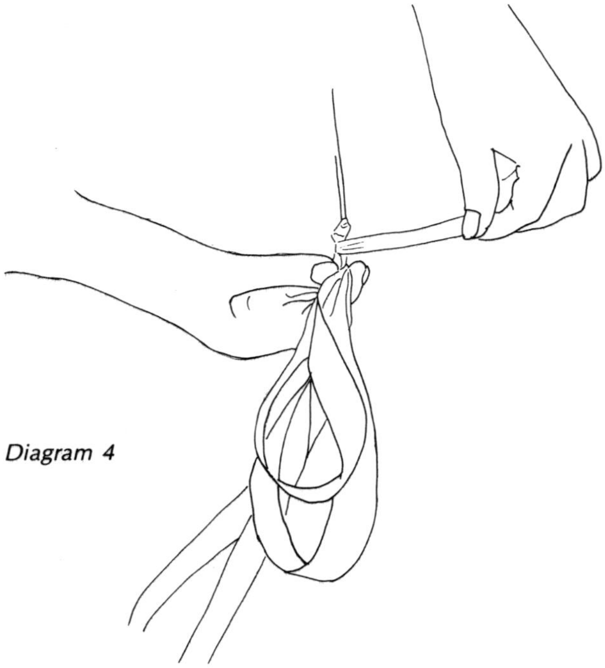

Diagram 4

Plain ribbon streamers

Materials
1.6 metres x 2 cm (1¾ yds) x 1'' ribbon
florist's tape
22 gauge florist's wire

Method
1. Follow the instructions above for the looped ribbon streamers.
2. Cut through the centre of each ribbon loop to give six ribbon strips. Cut the end of each strip at a 45^{0} angle. See diagram.

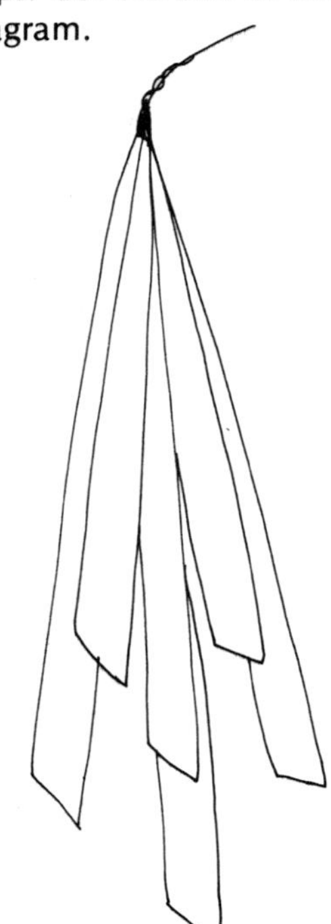

Three-loop ribbon bow

Materials
60 cm (24'') ribbon
22 gauge wire
florist's tape

Method
Loop the ribbon as in diagram 1. Gather the bottoms of the ribbon loops, place a 22 gauge wire with a hook at one end against the ribbon and twist tightly. See diagram 2. Tape to hide wire.

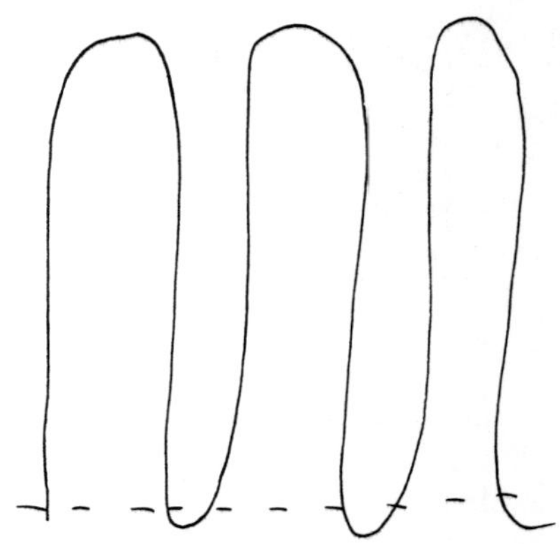

Diagram 1

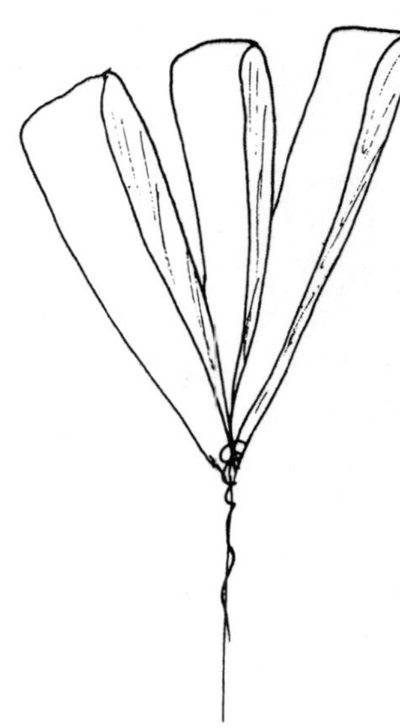

Diagram 2

Flowergirl's headband features pink and cream roses, gum leaves and dried baby's breath fixed to an Alice band (page 35)

The flowergirl's side comb is trimmed with pink flowers, baby's breath and gum leaves (page 36)

This bridal table arrangement is an attractive combination of white and apricot rosebuds, dried gum and baby's breath (page 48)

Simple guest table centrepiece (page 50)

Wedding cake top (page 47) and cake sprays (page 48) are dainty combinations of white and apricot mini rosebuds and forget-me-nots

Main picture:
A topiary tree of white roses and tufts of tulle is simplicity itself to make (page 45)

Generously-sized flower and tulle pew decoration (page 40)

Simple but effective, this pew bow is made of wide paper ribbon (page 45)

Six-loop ribbon bow

Materials
1 m (1¼ yds) ribbon
needle and cotton
22 gauge wire
florist's tape

Method
1. Loop ribbon as in diagram 1. With a loose running stitch gather up the centre, pull tight and secure.
2. Wrap the wire around the centre of the bow and twist tightly. Tape to hide wire. See diagrams 2 and 3.

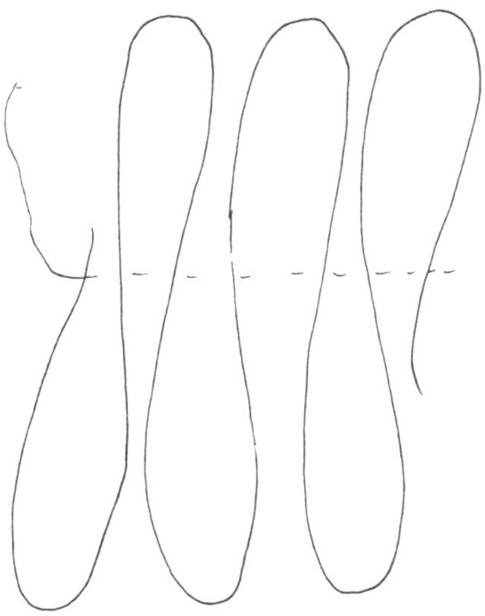

Diagram 1

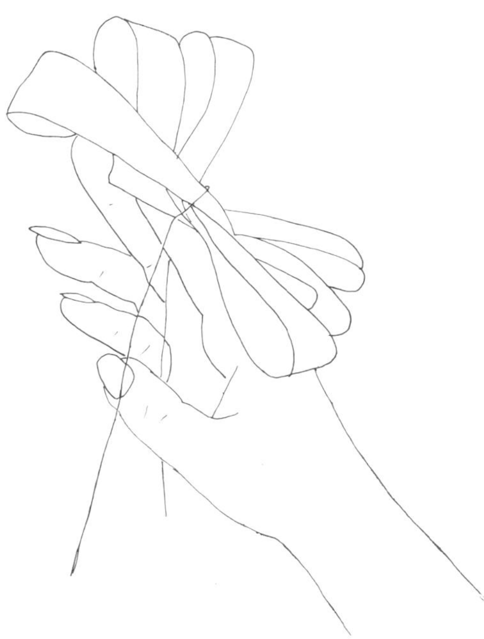

Diagram 2

Diagram 3

Satin bow for sheaf bouquet

Materials
50 cm x 115 cm (20'' x 45'') heavy satin
needle and cotton

Method
1. Following diagram 1 on the next page, cut two fabric pieces, 55 cm x 25 cm (22'' x 10'') and 45 cm x 20 cm (18'' x 8'').
2. Fold the larger piece of fabric lengthways so the raw edges meet in the centre, then press with a warm iron along the folded edges. Take the ends of the bow and bring them into the centre. Sew with gathering stitch, pull tight and secure. See diagram 2.
3. Repeat the above process with the smaller piece of fabric. Place the smaller bow on top of the larger bow and stitch together. See diagram 3.
4. To cover the centre of the bow cut a small piece of fabric 4 cm x 4 cm (1½'' x 1½''). Fold the raw edges into the centre lengthways and press with a warm iron. Wrap the fabric around the centre of the bow, fold one end under and stitch in place.
5. To make the bow trails cut two pieces of fabric 20 cm x 40 cm (8'' x 16'') as indicated in the layout in diagram 1. Fold fabric in half lengthways, wrong side out. Stitch down the non-folded side, following the dotted line in diagram 4. Cut away excess fabric, turn the trail to the right side and press with warm iron.
6. Gather in the tops of the bow trails and stitch them to the back of the bow. See diagram 5.

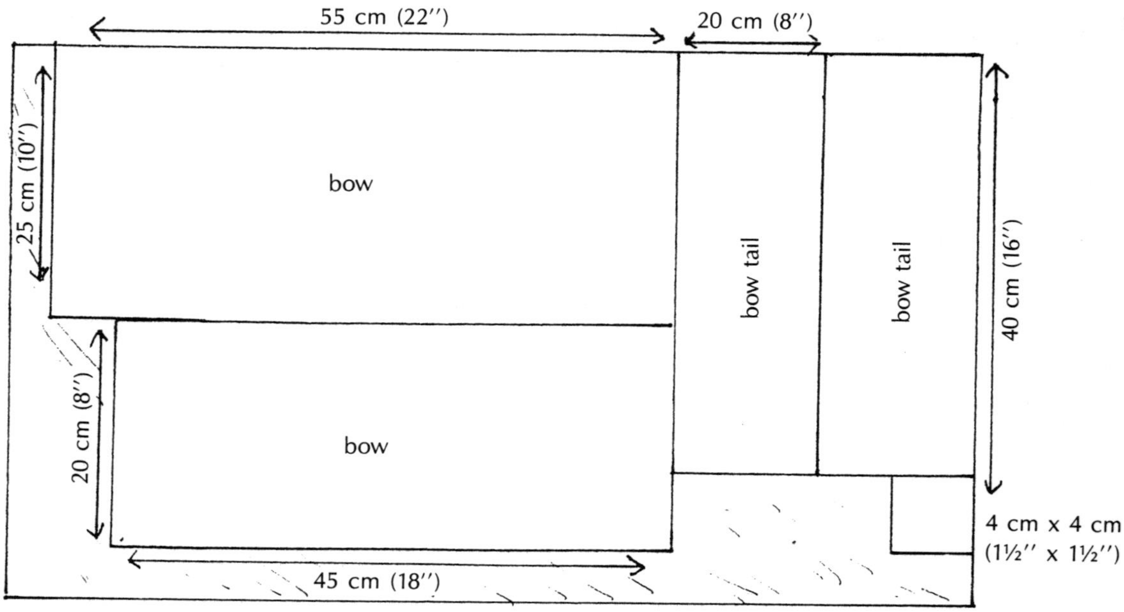

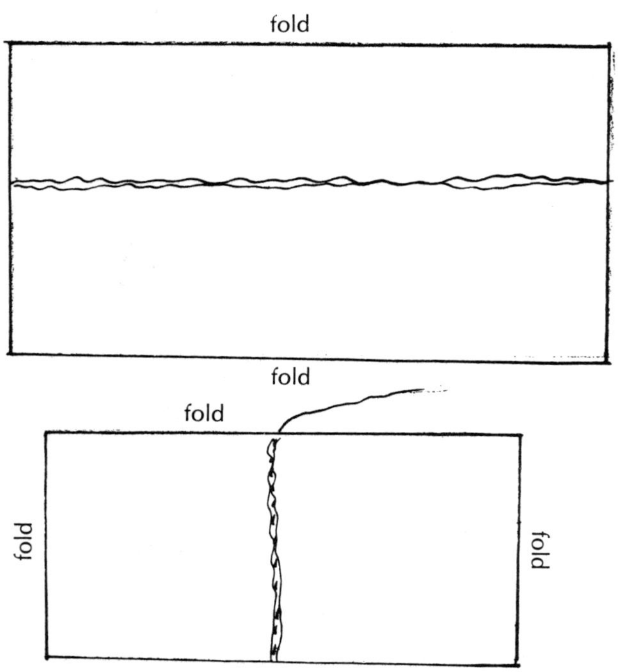

Diagram 2

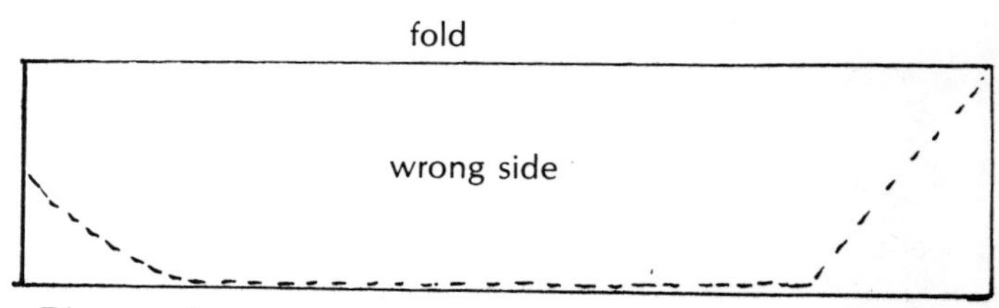

Diagram 4

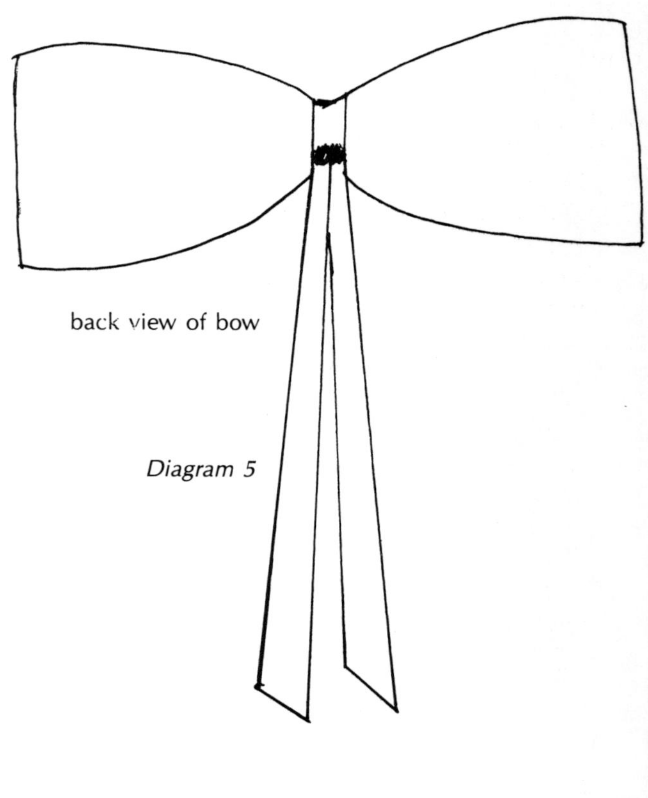

Diagram 5

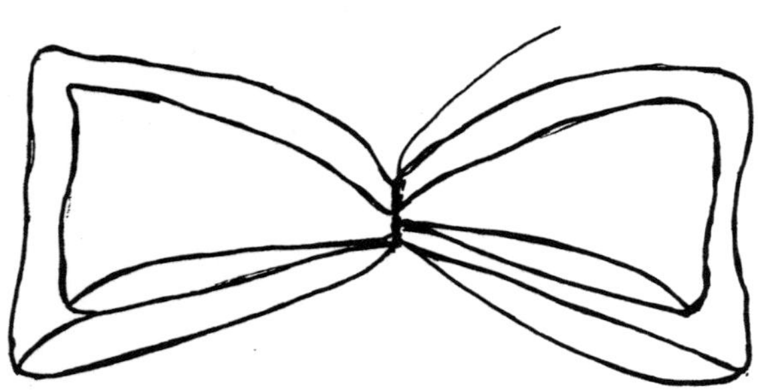

Diagram 3

Handmade roses

Today there are many products on the market which are excellent for handmade flowers. All are readily available at craft shops. The material I used in the handmade rose headpiece on page 32, called Model Magic, is available at art shops (see list of suppliers on page 63). The most inexpensive medium is bread dough.

Bread dough recipe
four slices white bread
PVA white glue

Method

1. Remove crusts from bread. Tear into small pieces, place in a bowl, add 1 tablespoon of PVA and mix. Remove from bowl and knead for 5-10 minutes or until it is pliable.
2. If the bread dough is too moist add a little more bread; if too dry add a little more glue.
3. Keep this material in Glad Wrap or a sealed container.

Materials for roses
modelling medium
24 gauge wire
folk art paint
small paint brush
florist's tape
Oasis

Method

1. To make the flowers, take a small amount of bread dough or other modelling medium about the size of a pea and flatten it out into a rounded rectangular shape. Take a 24 gauge wire with a hook at one end, lay it against the clay and roll the clay over the wire from right to left. See diagrams 1, 2 and 3.
2. Take another small piece of modelling clay, flatten it out fairly thinly to form a rough circle and wrap this around the bud to form a petal. Keep applying petals around the flower until you reach the desired size. See diagrams 4, 5 and 6.
3. If you find the base of the flower is getting too thick, just pinch away the excess.
4. Stand the wired flowers in a block of Oasis to dry for a day or so. When painting the flowers water the paint down so it won't be too thick and dark — you need to give the flowers just a hint of colour. If you want a deeper colour it is better to use three or four thin coats rather than one thick coat.
5. Finish off the flowers by taping the wire stems, starting just down from the base of the flower.

Note: Always keep modelling mediums wrapped in Glad Wrap or in a sealed container.

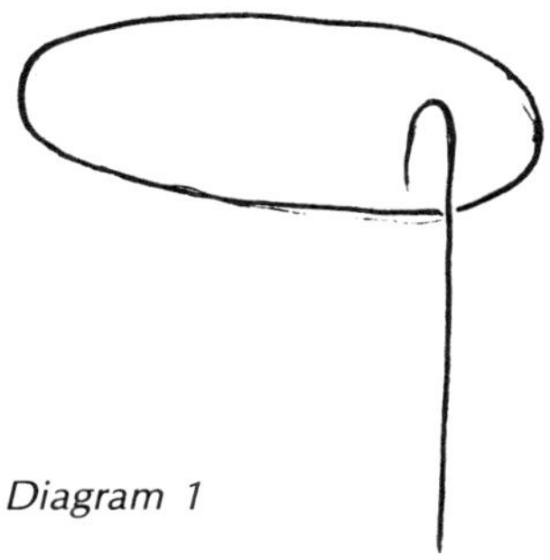

Diagram 1

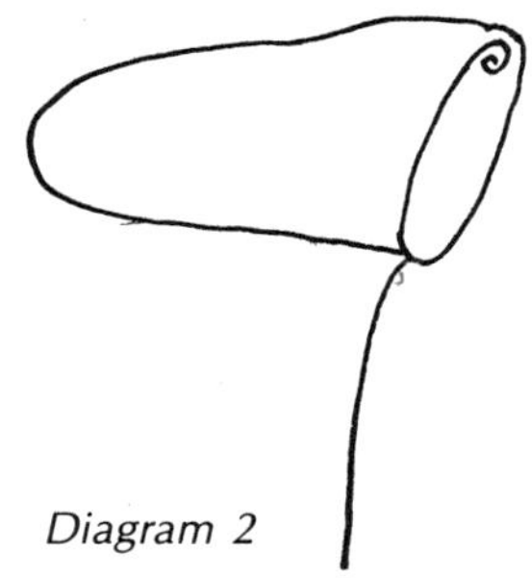

Diagram 2

Diagram 3

Diagram 4

Diagram 5

Diagram 6

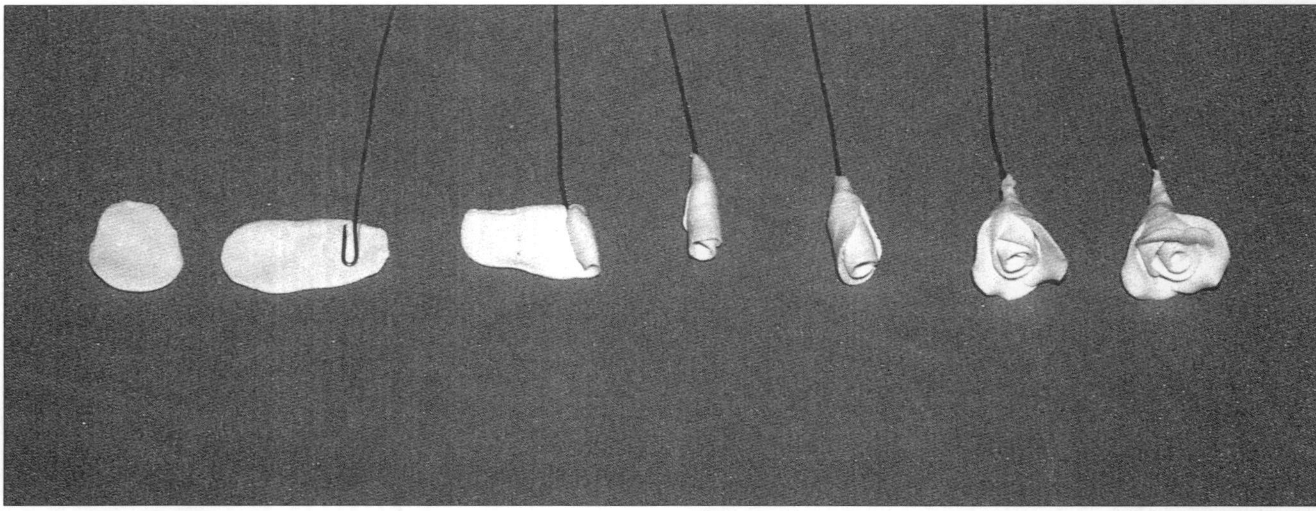

Steps in making handmade roses in modelling medium (see previous page)

Ribbon roses

Materials

3.5 m x 25 mm (4 yds x 1'') ribbon (makes 9 roses)
24 gauge wire
white florist's tape
needle and cotton

Method

1. Fold ribbon towards you at a 45º angle and lay a 24 gauge wire with hook at one end against the ribbon. See diagram 1.
2. Roll the ribbon over the wire from right to left two or three times then stitch to secure. See diagrams 2 and 3.
3. Fold ribbon back at a 45º angle and roll from right to left until you reach the lower left corner of the ribbon. See diagram 4.
4. Keep folding the ribbon back and rolling from right to left until you have a medium size rose. You might have to practice a few times, but remember they don't have to be perfect.
5. When you have about 3 cm (1½'') of ribbon left, fold the ribbon back, wrap it around the rose and stitch to secure (it might look a little untidy but don't worry). See diagram 6.
6. To tidy up the rose, cut away excess ribbon and bind the bottom of the rose and the wire with florist's tape. See diagram 7.

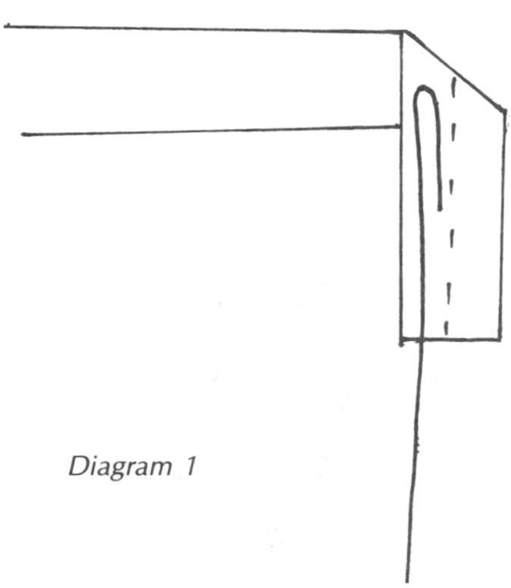

Diagram 1

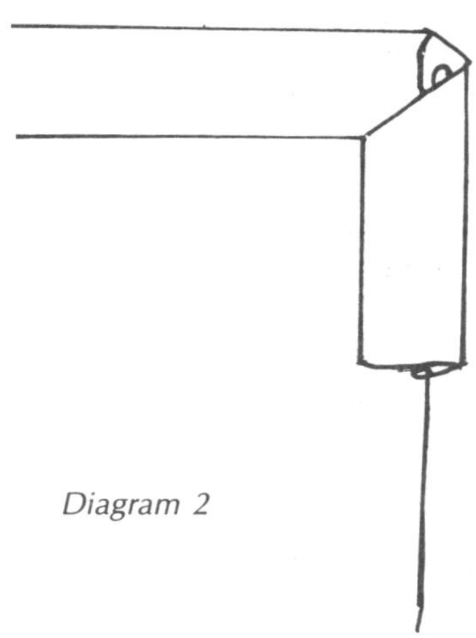

Diagram 2

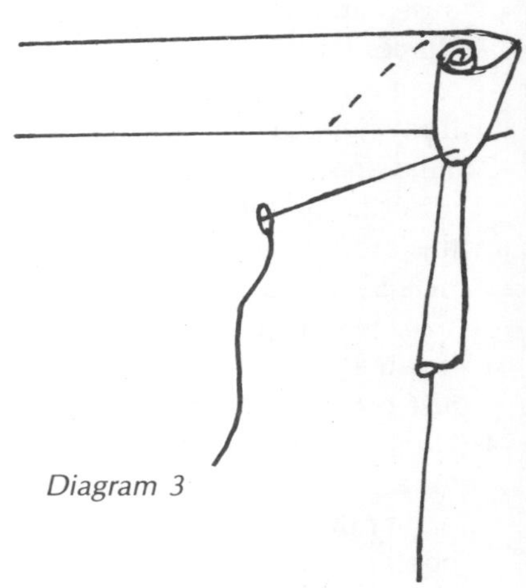

Diagram 3

Fabric leaves

Materials
25 cm (10'') silk fabric
26 gauge florist's wire
white florist's tape
needle and cotton

Method

1. Cut a square of fabric 8 cm x 8 cm (3'' x 3''). Fold corner to corner to make a triangle, then fold again to make a smaller triangle, pressing with a warm iron as you go.
2. Sew a running stitch along the non-folded edge. Insert a piece of wire with a hook at one end up through the centre of the leaf, then gather the stitching up tightly, twist the remaining cotton around the fabric and wire and secure with a few stitches. See diagrams 1 and 2.
3. To tidy up the stem cut away excess fabric and bind with florist's tape.

Diagram 4

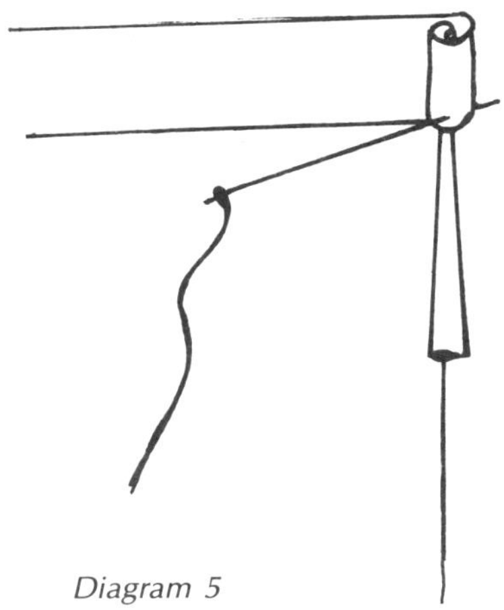

Diagram 5

Diagram 6

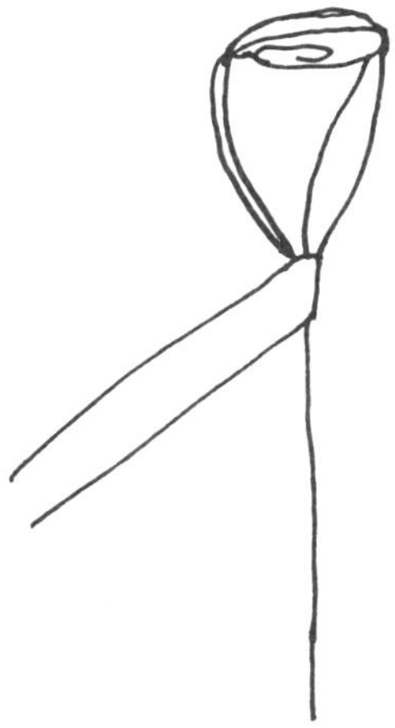

Diagram 7

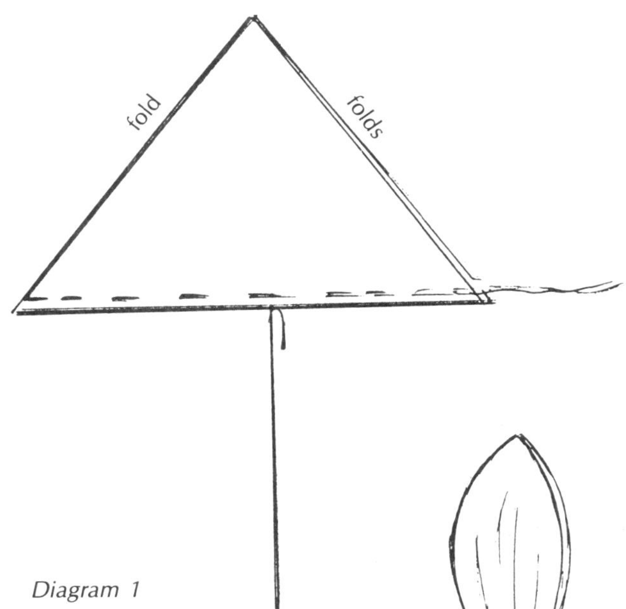

Diagram 1

Diagram 2

Small net tufts

Materials
1 m (1¼ yds) white net (makes 36 tufts)
22 gauge wire
white florist's tape
needle and cotton (optional)

Method
1. Cut four pieces of net 15 cm x 15 cm (6″ x 6″) and round the corners. With the four pieces laid one on top of the other run a gathering stitch across the centre of the net and secure. See diagram 1.
2. Wrap a 22 gauge wire around the gathered net and twist the longer wire around the shorter wire. See diagram 2.
3. The layers of net must now be separated. Pull each layer in opposite directions to fan the net out. See diagram 3.
4. To finish off, bind the wire with white florist's tape.

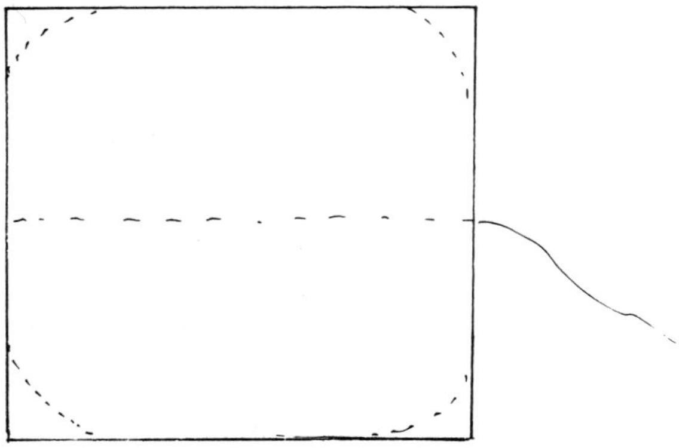

Diagram 1

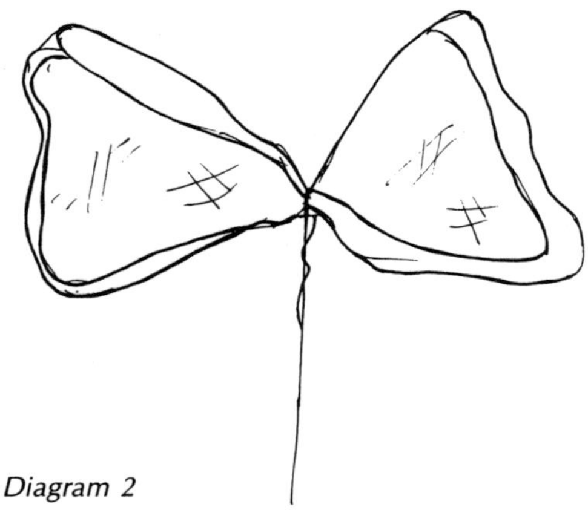

Diagram 2

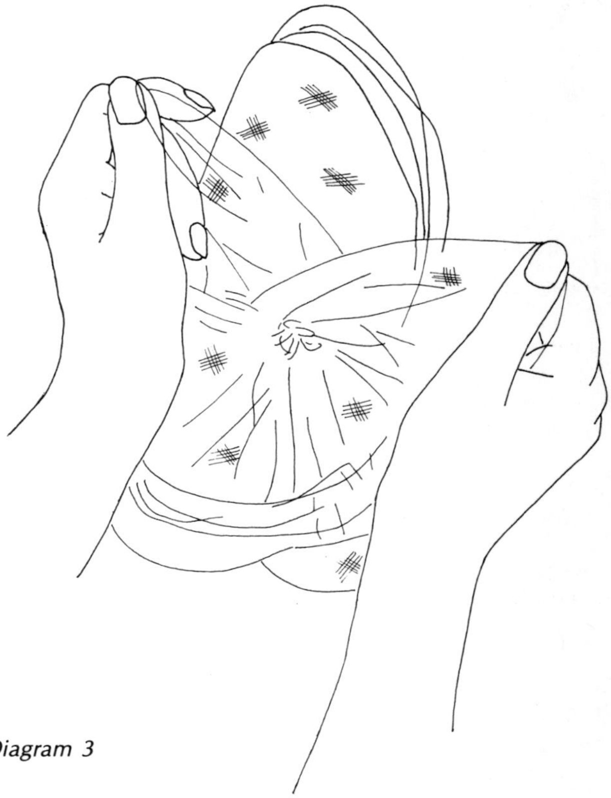

Diagram 3

Large net tufts

(see page 45)

Materials
1 m (1¼ yds) white net (makes 18 tufts)
22 gauge wire
needle and cotton

Method
1. Cut four pieces of net 36 cm x 15 cm (14¼″ x 6″) and round the corners. Lay the four pieces on top of each other, run a gathering stitch lengthwise up the centre of the net and secure.
2. Wrap a 22 gauge wire around the gathered net and bring the wires down together to the same length, twisting one around the other.
3. Separate the layers of net as shown in the previous instructions.
4. Taping the wire stems of these tufts is optional. Sometimes the tape is a hindrance when inserting the tufts into the Oasis of the topiary tree.

Suppliers

S.A.Brown Pty Ltd
52 Shepherd Street
Chippendale NSW 2008 (off Broadway)
(02) 699 7343

Flowerama
Unit 27, 8 Gladstone Road
Castle Hill NSW 2154
(02) 680 2320

Sydney's Dried Flower Barn
7 Bearing Road
Seven Hills NSW 2147
(02) 838 0385

C&S Imports
The Craft Warehouse
Shop 154 Warringah Mall
Brookvale NSW 2100
(02) 905 7072

Garndex Pty Ltd
Unit 3, 114 Station Road
Seven Hills NSW 2147
(02) 674 1199
(Open to the public Saturdays only,
9 am to 11 am)

Allis Wholesale Floral Supplies
11 Stanley Street
Peakhurst NSW 2210
(02) 584 1422

Hoxton Park Florist & Craft Supplies
Unit 13, 332 Hoxton Park Road
Hoxton Park NSW 2171
(02) 607 9840

Native Plants & Floral Supplies
155 Taren Point Road
Taren Point NSW 2229
(02) 526 1533

Bibi's Floral Supplies
41 York Road
Penrith NSW 2750
(047) 31 2109

Blooms & Nuts
8 Moore Street
Birmingham Gardens NSW 2287
(049) 51 7119

Floral Design Centre
26 Belmore Street
Wollongong NSW 2500
(042) 26 6574

J.M.Merchandise
6-8 Marshall Road
Dapto NSW 2530
(042) 62 1777

Petal Flora
Fyshwick Markets
Fyshwick ACT 2609
(06) 295 8121

Spotlight Stores (all states)
Head Office (03) 690 8899

Lincraft Stores (all states)
Head Office (03) 329 0320

Fabric Barn and Loft
30 William Street
Gosford NSW 2250
(043) 25 1104

Home Yardage
cnr. Church & Macquarie Streets
Parramatta NSW 2150
(02) 635 6399

Home Yardage
66 York Street
Sydney NSW 2000
(02) 290 3600

Cyril Preston Pty Ltd
258 Flinders Lane
Melbourne Vic. 3000
(03) 654 7062

JB Floral & Craft Supplies
Unit 2, 11 Pilgram Court
Ringwood Vic. 3134
(03) 872 3400

Flower World
12 Sara Grove
Tottenham Vic. 3012
(03) 315 2388

Millinery Warehouse
94 Welsby Place
New Farm Qld 4005
(07) 358 3511

Flower Factory
8 Trade Street
Cleveland Qld 4163
(07) 821 0244

Homework Handicraft
Shop 5, 615 North East Street
Gillies Plains SA 5086
(08) 26 6401

Meg Sheen Craftsman Supplies
308 Hay Street
Subiaco WA 6008
(09) 381 8215

Gilberts Bridal & Floral Handicrafts
306 Murray Street (basement level)
Perth WA 6000
(09) 321 9873

Most craft shops and florist's shops
carry floral supplies.

Suppliers for
MODEL MAGIC MODELLING CLAY

Deans Art Supplies
21 Atchison Street
St Leonards NSW 2065
(02) 439 4944

Artistcare
93 York Street
Sydney NSW 2000
(02) 299 4151

Artistcare
2-8 Phillip Street
Parramatta NSW 2150
(02) 893 9191

Melbourne Handcrafts
(03) 882 8833
(City, Southlands, Northlands, Camberwell, Chadstone, Doncaster, Frankston)

One Stop Art
1053 Burwood Highway
Ferntree Gully Vic. 3156
(03) 752 2722

Artistcare
65 Mary Street
Brisbane Qld 4000
(07) 210 0566

Sundale Handcrafts
Shop 315 Australia Fair
Scarborough Street
Southport Qld 4215
(075) 32 2204

Miart
57 East Street
Rockhampton Qld 4700
(079) 22 5040

Duthy Street Art
4-6 Duthy Street
Unley SA 5061
(08) 373 3314

Artistcare
214 Gouger Street
Adelaide SA 5000
(08) 211 8883

Jackson's RT
108 Beaufort Street
Northbridge WA 6000
(09) 328 8880

Index